From Saginaw Valley to Tin Pan Alley

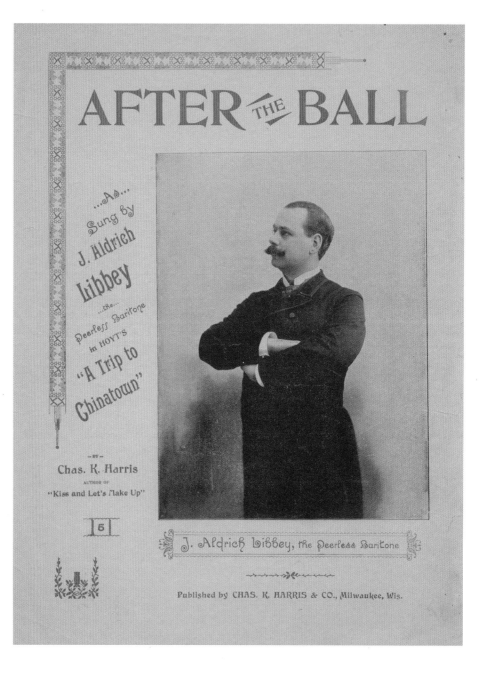

Figure 1. The 1892 hit "After the Ball," which marked the beginning of the Tin Pan Alley area, was written by Charles K. Harris, who grew up in Saginaw, Michigan.

From Saginaw Valley to Tin Pan Alley

Saginaw's Contribution to
American Popular Music,
1890-1955

R. GRANT SMITH

 Wayne State University Press • Detroit

GREAT LAKES BOOKS

A complete listing of the books in this series
can be found at the back of this volume.

Philip P. Mason, Editor
Department of History, Wayne State University

Dr. Charles K. Hyde, Associate Editor
Department of History, Wayne State University

Library of Congress Cataloging-in-Publication Data

Smith, R. Grant, 1931–
      From Saginaw Valley to Tin Pan Alley : Saginaw's contribution to
   American popular music, 1890–1955 / R. Grant Smith.
          p.   cm. — (Great Lakes books)
      Includes bibliographical references (p.   ) and index.
      ISBN 0-8143-2658-7 (pbk. : alk. paper)
      1. Popular music—Michigan—Saginaw—History and criticism
   I. Title.   II. Series
   ML3477.8.S24S65   1998
   782.42164'0977'46—dc21   97-14036

This book is dedicated to my parents, Bob and Gladdie Smith, who, together, experienced the Tin Pan Alley years firsthand. They listened to many of the wonderful songs of the era; they danced to some of them; and, sometimes, when they didn't know anyone else could hear, they even sang a few of the songs—to each other.

CONTENTS

List of Color Illustrations

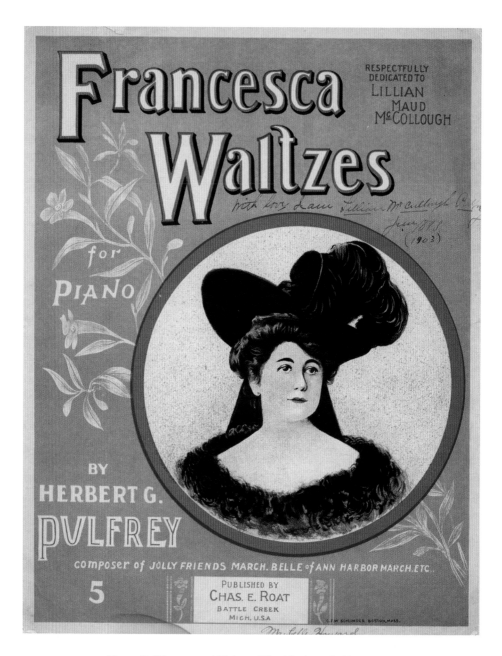

Figure 2. "Francesca Waltzes," by Herbert Pulfrey, was written in 1902, just before he moved to Saginaw.

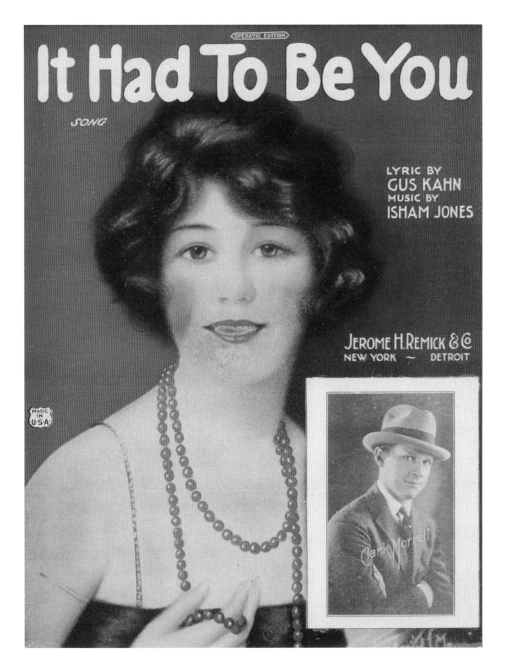

Figure 3. One of the best-known songs of the Tin Pan Alley years was Isham Jones's 1924 hit, "It Had to Be You."

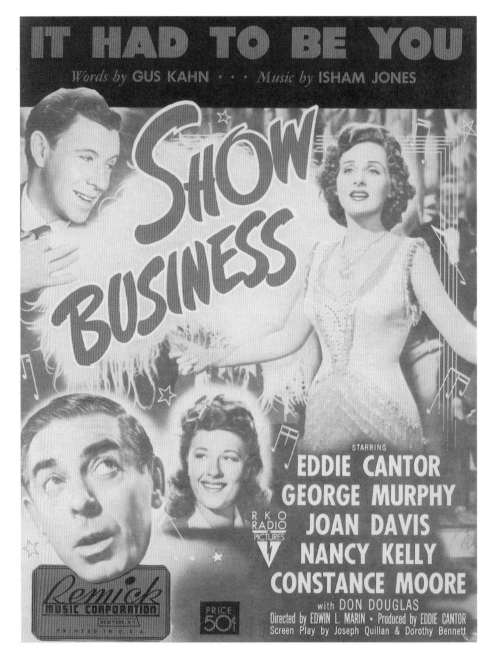

Figure 4. A later edition of "It Had to Be You" was published in 1944.

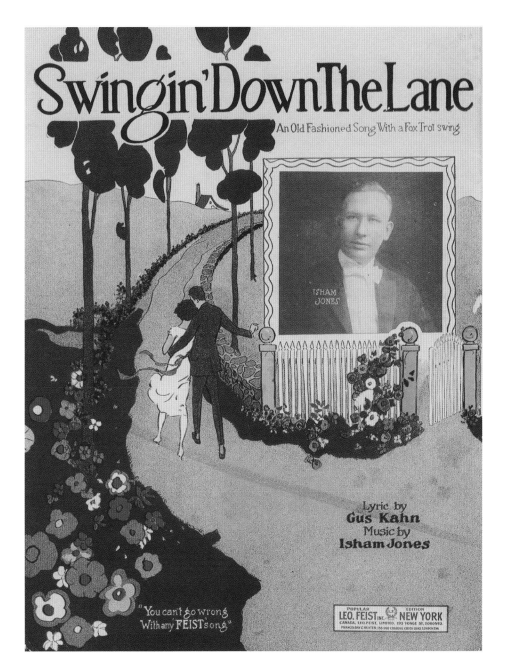

Figure 5. Isham Jones's sentimental hit, "Swingin' down the Lane," was written in 1923.

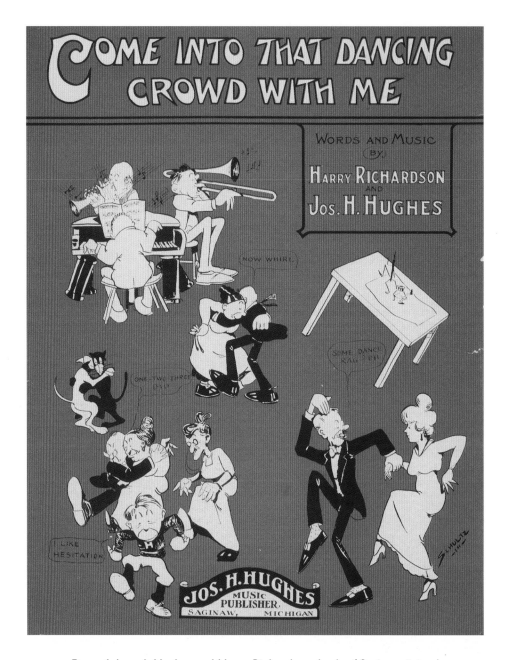

Figure 6. Joseph Hughes and Harry Richardson, both of Saginaw, joined forces to write "Come into That Dancing Crowd with Me" in 1914.

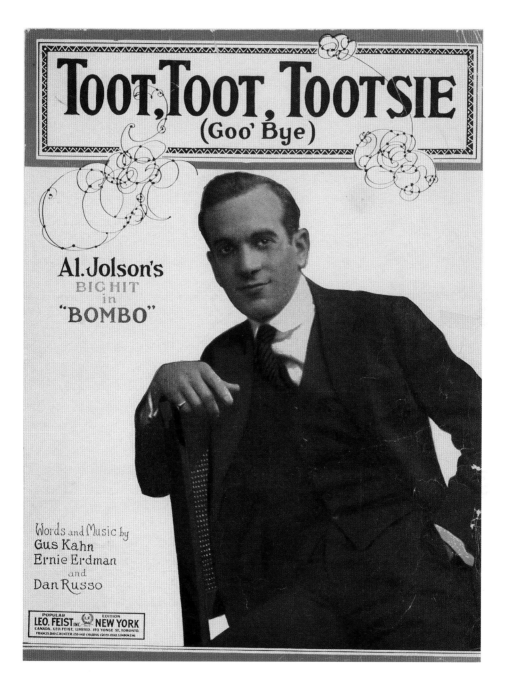

Figure 7. Dan Russo's big hit, "Toot, Toot, Tootsie, Goo'Bye," was written in 1921.

Figure 8. Isham Jones composed "Spain" in 1924 on the same night he wrote "The One I Love Belongs to Somebody Else" and "It Had to Be You."

Figure 9. "Lovely Lady" was written by Carl Rupp in 1924.

Figure 10. One of Carl Rupp's dance hits,
"The Black Pigeon Wing," was written in 1929.

FOREWORD

Few people realize that the start and subsequent growth of Tin Pan Alley, the once-famous dream street of musical success, has a connection to Saginaw, Michigan.

But the connection is there, as Grant Smith shows in his delightful and beautifully written book. Why Saginaw became part of the story of Tin Pan Alley is going to cause a lot of people to rush to a map to find out where Saginaw is located. For those that do not know, it is just west of Michigan's Thumb, on the Saginaw River.

Saginaw turned out many musical geniuses. Such giants as Charles Harris, Isham Jones, Danny Russo, and Gerald Marks all came from Saginaw. They were only the best known; the list of lesser-known songwriters is long and cataloged in an appendix.

Why Saginaw turned out so many talented musicians is a question that has concerned every historian of the city. Saginaw was once known across the United States and beyond as one of the lumber capitals of the world from about 1850 to 1900. After the Civil War, Michigan white pine helped rebuild the destroyed nation. Saginaw was the center of this often wild, rough, and brutal period.

Perhaps there was something in the air in Saginaw that created an individualism in people, a freedom of expression that encouraged and nurtured talent.

The free-wheeling lumberjacks came to Saginaw looking for entertainment and excitement. They found it in the saloons that operated freely, unchecked by a city government that believed, "If we don't provide what the lumberjacks want, somebody else will." City leaders did not want all of that nice money that jingled in the lumberjacks' pockets to go elsewhere.

The reason for Saginaw's concentration of talent may never be discovered. Maybe there was something like footlight fever in the great piles of sawdust that lined the river. It was not only expressed in music. Marie Dressler (then known as Lila Koerber) got her stage start in Saginaw. Tim

McCoy, one of the first popular cowboys, was the son of a Saginaw police chief who grew up watching his father deal with rowdy lumberjacks. The area also produced a great boxer: George Lavigne, the famous Saginaw Kid, who was lightweight champion of the world from 1893 to 1899.

Grant has documented the musical greats of Tin Pan Alley. It is about time the world, and Saginaw, too, for that matter, realized the tunes that delighted them at dances once upon a time came out of Saginaw. Just to know that "All of Me," "It Had to Be You," "Sleepy Time Gal," "Toot, Toot, Tootsie, Goo'Bye," "I'll See You in My Dreams," and "Is It True What They Say About Dixie?" have a Saginaw connection is enough to make a Saginaw resident feel proud.

Stuart Gross

ACKNOWLEDGMENTS

Many people have contributed, in one way or another, to making this book what it is—a study of Saginaw's place in the popular music of America. Special recognition must be given to three people who have been responsible for some of the material that appears in these pages: journalist Stuart Gross and songwriters Ben Weisman and Gerald Marks. Without their help, this study would not be complete.

I also wish to express my gratitude to the following individuals for their valuable contributions: George Anderson, Betty Baxter, Jerry Bhirdo, Dr. Allen P. Britton, Bill Brown, Geraldine Brown, Pat Burbott, Dorothy Campbell, Paul Daines, Laura Lee Ewald, Catherine Faunce, Robert Grant, Sue Grant, Chuck Hoover, Bill Kempf, Marty Kempf, Marie Laeding, Lori Lee, Judy Leece, Dorothy Lingenfelter, Peggy Lugthart, Ruth Ann Lundgren, Anna Mae Maday, Doris Marsh, Laura McDonald, Bob McIntyre, Bill Miles, Grace Norris, Bill Oberschmidt, Marvel Hodge Patton, Mary Phillips, Ruth Picard, Ronald Putz, Jerry Roe, Dr. Robert Roeser, Jim Romaker, Dr. Calvin Schorer, Elaine Schwanbeck, Junior Schwanbeck, Mike Slasinski, Gloria P. Soughan, Jack Tucker, Howard Vasold, Jim Vervoort, Mary Way, Diane Woodworth, and Dr. William Woodworth. Last, and far from least, there are two ladies whose patience and forgiveness have been severely and repeatedly tested throughout the writing of this book. My deepest appreciation goes to my typist/computer operator, Marguerite McIntyre, and to my wife, Mary Ann Smith.

INTRODUCTION

In 1982, I was delighted to receive an invitation to make a presentation in conjunction with Saginaw Valley State University's Humanities Series. The topic I was asked to address was Saginaw's contribution to American popular music, focusing on both the music itself and the people who wrote it. This subject is a great favorite of mine, so soon after I received the invitation, I was happily engrossed in collecting relevant information and material.

After completing much of the necessary research, I realized that presenting a program that consisted merely of facts and dates would do little to stimulate audience interest. The presentation would be far more effective if some of the songs were performed. So, with assistance from singer Jerry Bhirdo, the program was prepared and presented. We were even able to get Saginaw songwriter Gerald Marks to put in an appearance that evening.

Recently it occurred to me that it might be interesting to put together a similar presentation, this time in print, which would include much of the material that was presented for the Humanities Series program, but which would be expanded considerably to include additional information about Saginaw's many songwriters and their astonishing output of successful popular songs. I also felt that readers who enjoy the artwork or graphic design of sheet music covers of the Tin Pan Alley era might find those with a Saginaw connection of interest. I have tried to include illustrations of the covers of the best-known songs, as well as those that reflect the history of the time, are aesthetically pleasing, or are just plain interesting.

Information and materials for this book were collected through extensive research in a number of scholarly and popular publications, countless visits to antique shops and antique shows (sorting through literally hundreds of thousands of pieces of sheet music), and personal interviews with songwriters from Saginaw and others familiar with Saginaw's contributions to the music of Tin Pan Alley. Every effort was made to obtain permission to print illustrations of the sheet music covers included here.

Conceding the fact that there is nothing quite so good as actually hearing the songs played and sung, I hope that readers will still enjoy learning about Saginaw's remarkable place in American popular music. It is my hope, too, that the material presented here will enhance readers' enjoyment of listening to these songs.

1

⊠　⊠　⊠

SETTING THE STAGE

THINK ABOUT THIS LIST OF PEOPLE: an automobile dealer, a department store window trimmer, a playwright, a stenographer, a bellboy, an insurance salesman, a vaudeville performer, a federal judge, a movie theater owner, a draftsman, and a mule team driver. It is hard to imagine a more diverse group, yet these people had two things in common—they all lived in Saginaw at one time, and they all wrote songs that made an impact on popular music in the United States between 1890 and 1955. How and why so many talented songwriters came from a single community in Michigan is a story few know.

The Saginaw Valley is flat piece of real estate in central Michigan. The city of Saginaw is located in its approximate center. The region has some excellent farmland on which is raised a variety of crops, mainly beans and sugar beets. Although the principal industries in the area now include the manufacture of automobiles and chemicals, it was not always the case.

In the 1870s and 1880s, the Saginaw Valley was covered with forests of pine and Saginaw was the center of a huge lumbering industry. The trees were felled, cut into logs, and floated down the Saginaw River to the many sawmills that lined its shores. There the logs were cut into standard lumber sizes and delivered to nearby Saginaw Bay, where the lumber was loaded on ships and sent to ports all over the world.

After most of the trees had been cut down and the lumber industry gradually gave way to other types of commerce, especially a burgeoning automobile manufacturing industry, the populace of the region took on a much more cosmopolitan outlook. Whereas the earlier population had been comprised primarily of loggers and a few Native Americans, people from many other occupations and ethnic origins began moving into the area, bringing with them new cultural standards and value systems, including new tastes in entertainment.

As Saginaw and the communities around it grew and as people from diverse backgrounds became more accustomed to living together and working together, mutually acceptable goals and standards developed. Public taste gradually assimilated a number of common elements which helped form the basis for a shared outlook on music in the area. This, in turn, gave rise to a generation or two of prolific and influential popular songwriters.

Some of these songwriters were not born in Saginaw, but almost all of them grew up there, absorbing both the formal and informal musical influences the community had to offer. In Saginaw their ideas and feelings for music were formed and developed, to be expressed eventually in thousands of songs that the people in America and elsewhere came to know and love. The music these Saginaw composers and lyricists wrote was the right thing at the right time, and it helped entertain the listening and dancing public from the nineteenth century to the post–World War II era. Of course, other areas also produced composers and lyricists who helped shape the popular music scene during these decades, but this book is concerned with the music and the lives of these songwriters who lived in Saginaw. This work traces the evolution of the music created by these songwriters between 1890 and 1955, taking note of how the melodic, harmonic, and rhythmic nature of the music changed through the years, and at how the lyrics reflected the history and moods of the times in which they were written.

On a summer day in New York City, just before 1900, songwriter and journalist Monroe Rosenfeld walked down West 28th Street, on the way to his publisher, to demonstrate a new song he had written. As he passed the rows of music publishing houses, clustered together and piled on top of each other, he heard the sounds of hundreds of pianos, playing hundreds of pieces of music, pouring out of the open windows. The tumultuous noise reminded him of tin pans clanging together.

Later that day, when Rosenfeld returned to his typewriter at the *New York Herald,* he wrote an article about what he had just experienced, referring to the area he had visited as "Tin Pan Alley." This name would remain synonymous with the popular music publishing industry in America for the next sixty years. "Tin Pan Alley" would also serve as a sobriquet for the style of American popular music written during this period.

The Tin Pan Alley era thrived on the talents of many of the greatest songwriters the world has ever known. Some of the top lyricists of this period were Sammy Cahn, Howard Dietz, Al Dubin, Ray Egan, Dorothy Fields, Ira Gershwin, Oscar Hammerstein II, Lorenz Hart, Gus Kahn, Bert Kalmer, Alan Jay Lerner, Frank Loesser, Johnny Mercer, and Mitchell Parish. Among the great Tin Pan Alley composers were Harold Arlen, Hoagy Carmichael, Walter Donaldson, Vernon Duke, Duke Ellington, George Gershwin, Isham Jones, Jerome Kern, Jimmy McHugh, Richard Rodgers, Harry Ruby, Arthur Schwartz, Jule Styne, Jimmy VanHeusen, Harry Warren, Richard Whiting, and Vincent Youmans. A few Tin Pan Alley songwriters, such as Irving Berlin, George M. Cohan, and Cole Porter, wrote both words and music. These people, along with many others—some from Saginaw—provided America and the rest of the world with popular music for well over sixty years.

Sadly, Tin Pan Alley no longer exists. The post–World War II era brought many changes to popular culture, not the least of which was the direction popular music took. The American teenager and even the pre-teenager became powerful forces to be reckoned with in the commercial music market. The great melodic, harmonic, and rhythmic variety that for so long had characterized American popular music rapidly gave way to rock and pop songs that often employed few chords, and whose repetitious melodies, rhythms, and lyrics spoke resoundingly of a far less sophisticated buying public.[1] Rather than dwell on the demise of Tin Pan Alley, however, let us take a good look at that institution—its roots and its growth—and at the Saginaw songwriters who contributed so generously to its extraordinary success.

---

1. "The popular music of Tin Pan Alley had something to offer people of all ages, whereas the appeal of rock music has generally been aimed at young people," celebrating what sociologist turned music critic Howard Husock calls "youthful excesses and alienation." According to Husock, "The overwhelming influence of rock on today's popular music leaves the young with neither the steadying influence of a tale of personal experience nor the sense of belonging to a national culture, which pop music has historically transmitted." Howard Husock, "Popular Song," *Wilson Quarterly* (Summer 1988).

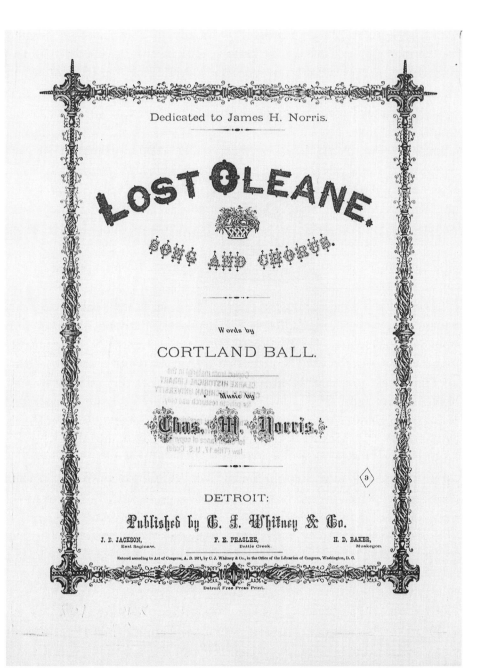

Charles Norris's "Lost Oleane," written in 1871, was one of the first songs published by a Saginaw resident.

2

◨   ◨   ◨

BEFORE THE ALLEY

THERE WERE SOME SAGINAW COMPOSERS AND MUSIC TEACHERS who preceded the Tin Pan Alley era who deserve to be recognized for their work in laying the foundation for what was to follow. The earliest of these was Charles Merrill Norris. He was born in Bradley, Maine, in 1849. Norris moved to Saginaw at an early age and, eventually, ran a music dealership there which, by the 1880s, became the largest in central Michigan.

In 1870, Norris wrote a piece of music called "Lonely Hours—An Original Theme with Variations" and dedicated it to Mrs. Abbie D. Norris, his mother. This piece, printed by C. J. Whitney and Company of Detroit, was the earliest published secular composition from the Saginaw area. Norris followed this work with "Lost Oleane" in 1871 and "Dreamland Wanderings" in 1872. In 1875, he composed "Don Quixote March" and in 1877, "The Red Ribbon March." The latter bore the inscription, "Most sincerely dedicated to the members of the Saginaw Red Ribbon Club." (The Red Ribbon Club was a national temperance organization that pitted its energies locally against those of the hard-drinking lumberjacks and other imbibing members of the community.)

Norris also wrote "The No Name Waltz" in 1885, "East Saginaw Grand March" (probably in 1888), and "Aristocracy Waltzes" in 1895. He further distinguished himself by being the father of two of Saginaw's other pre–Tin Pan Alley songwriters, Alfred W. Norris and Harold J. Norris.

Other very early songwriters in Saginaw were Saleu L. Tyler, J. Van Loon, Thomas C. Roney, Henry B. Roney, and H. C. Cabot.[1] Tyler's "Only a Brook" was published in East Saginaw in 1872 by Tyler Bros. and Company, a small music dealership. Van Loon's "Bootblack's Whistle Waltz" and Thomas Roney's "Psi Upsilon Waltzes" both came out in 1875. Henry Roney's "Rifle Waltzes" (dedicated to the East Saginaw Rifles) and Cabot's "Capitol Guards Polka and Mazurka" were published the following year.[2] All of the pieces mentioned so far, with the exception of Charles Norris's first three songs and Tyler's composition, were published by A. W. Wheat and Company of East Saginaw. Wheat was Norris's business partner in the large music dealership that Norris eventually took over and expanded.

In 1894, Alfred Norris turned out a song called "The Krinolin Two-Step," which became quite popular for a while. This song was published by his father's music center. The front page of the piece displayed an ad that read, "as played by the leading bands and orchestras everywhere." Advertising was starting to become important to songwriters and to the music publishing industry.

Judging by the titles of two of Alfred Norris's other songs, he may have been an early advocate of equal rights for women. One of these was "Twentieth-Century Woman." The other, "Fair Detective," was a march from a musical play, *The Wrong Mr. Wright,* in which Isadore Rush played the role of a woman detective. On the back page of "Fair Detective" are advertisements for "The Krinolin Two-Step" and "Twentieth-Century Woman." These ads, hardly characterized by excessive modesty, describe Norris's songs as "Decided and original hits! Striking, Catchy, Brilliant, they have pleased the ear of thousands and thousands. Played by Sousa's, Gilmore's, Liberati's, Brooks's, and other famous bands, and all the theater orchestras in the United States. Sales have been enormous." Norris wrote a number of other songs, including an 1898 composition titled "Saginaw Carnival March," which he "Respectfully dedicated to the Street Fair and Carnival committee."[3]

---

1. Tyler, Van Loon, the Roneys, and the Norrises all lived in Saginaw. Nothing is known about Cabot, other than the fact that he wrote this piece of music and published it in Saginaw. It is assumed that he was a resident of the Saginaw area because most songwriters had their work published near where they lived, as a matter of convenience. There were publishers in many other communities; if Cabot had lived elsewhere, he probably would have engaged the services of another publisher.

2. On the front cover of this piece are small portraits of the men who, apparently, comprised that committee: W. M. Turner, D. E. Prall, Thomas A. Downs, Captain A. L. Button, and Saginaw Mayor William A. Baum.

3. Besides being a successful songwriter, Alfred Norris was also Saginaw's first automobile dealer. In this capacity, he sold one of the first cars ever purchased in Saginaw, a used 1903 Oldsmobile. (It is interesting to speculate as to where Norris, or anyone, for that matter, could find a used car at that time.)

Harold J. Norris, who worked at the Norris Music House in Saginaw, also did a little songwriting around the turn of the century. In 1900, he teamed up with his brother (Alfred wrote the music and Harold the lyrics) to compose "A Little Brunette Dressed in Pink." Another song that Harold wrote by himself a few years later, "The Home Comers March and Two-Step," enjoyed popularity in the Saginaw area for some time.

In 1890, Saginaw music dealer Frank H. Erd composed and published "Erd's Music House Schottische." This composition was probably more a commercial venture than a musical one: the first and last pages contain a considerable amount of advertising; for example, "Go to Erd for pianos, organs, and all kinds of musical instruments . . . sold on easy monthly payments. Old instruments taken in exchange. 10,000 copies of standard sheet music, only 10 cents a copy. Catalogue mailed on application." Showing the broad interests of many early composers, Erd had, at various times in his brief life (he died at age thirty-three) worked as a machinist, a performing musician, a music teacher, and a pianomaker.

Charles B. Schaefer was a well-known journalist in the Saginaw area from about 1885 until his death in 1903. He served as editor-in-chief of the *Saginaw Globe,* and later published the *Michigan Miner.* In 1894 he composed and published a piece of music called "The Devil's Delight."

Louis C. Toepel was a music teacher who lived and taught in Saginaw. He wrote a number of songs, including the words and music to an 1894 ballad, "Your Mother's Heart." An article that appeared in the *Saginaw Globe* that year described this piece as "a very pleasing, sentimental song . . . with a pleasing melody, well designed to meet public favor. The words . . . contain a pleasing sentiment." The phrase "well designed to meet public favor" was of great significance. This concept would become the basis for the success of the popular music publishing industry throughout the Tin Pan Alley era and later.

Pianist Harry Turner lived in Saginaw for a few years during the mid 1890s. In 1894, he composed "Light Infantry March and Two-Step" and dedicated it to the Saginaw Light Infantry. This piece, perhaps meant for dances sponsored by the local militia unit, is more of a dance, as the last part of its title indicates, than a military march. Turner used both major and minor keys in the various sections of the piece, and the transitions he employed made it obvious he was comfortable moving adeptly from one key to another. The piece is typical of the Victorian period, yet the melodies Turner used were quite lyrical for a march, and they hinted at the style of the wonderful melodies that would soon characterize the Tin Pan Alley years.

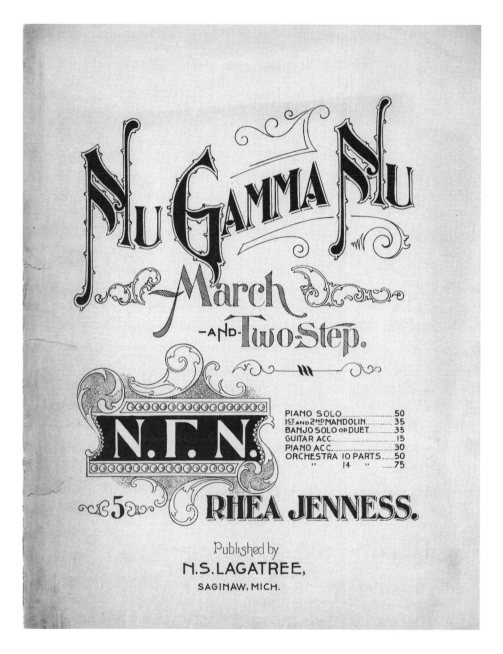

"Nu Gamma Nu March and Two-Step" was composed by Rhea Jenness in 1900. Arrangements were printed for a variety of instruments.

Advertisements like this often appeared on the pages of early sheet music.

In 1897, Napoleon S. Lagatree, a Saginaw music teacher, wrote "In Idle Moments," to be played on "the Banjo, Mandolin and Guitar." This song was published by Barrows Music Company of Saginaw. Lagatree also wrote a number of other instrumental selections and a teaching method for banjo.

Just as Thomas C. Roney had done twenty-five years earlier, Saginaw native Rhea Jenness wrote a piece honoring one of the many Greek

Herbert Pulfrey's "Caroline" was published in 1906 by
the Peerless Music Publishing Company of Saginaw.

letter societies, "Nu Gamma Nu March and Two-Step." This work was published in Saginaw by Napoleon Lagatree in 1900.

In 1907, Herbert G. Pulfrey, an insurance agent who had moved to Saginaw from Battle Creek, wrote a highly spirited piece titled "Red Hots," which was published by Peerless Music of Saginaw. Billed as a march and two-step, this song is characterized throughout by syncopated rhythms which reflect the period's growing influence of ragtime. Pulfrey also wrote several other songs that enjoyed some local acclaim, including one in 1909 titled "The Cable March and Two-Step," which he dedicated to the Cable Piano Company of Chicago. In addition to advertisements for several models of Cable pianos, the pages of this composition carry ads for Edison phonographs and records, and for "Century Edition Standard and Popular Sheet Music by All the Famous Composers." It, too, was published by the Peerless Music Publishing Company.

This piece of music is particularly interesting because in 1903, Lou H. Dockstader, who was not from Saginaw, had composed a work titled "The Cable March and Two-Step," which had been published by the Cable Piano Company and bears a large ad for Cable pianos on its back cover. Although the melodies, harmonies, and key signatures of these two pieces are different, they feature similar rhythms and identical forms, as indicated by their common title. Each bears a valid copyright. Perhaps the Cable Piano Company did much of its advertising by encouraging local composers to glorify its name.

Louis Harold Wondree, a Saginaw music teacher, wrote "The Gallant Brigade" in 1914. This piece was a "military march and two-step," a form and style of music that had been in vogue since the 1860s, but which by 1914 was fading from popularity. A comparison of "The Gallant Brigade" with Pulfrey's "Red Hots" shows how much the musical styles of different periods overlap.

Elmer E. Fogg was born in Ann Arbor in 1861, but later moved to Saginaw and established himself as a well-known and respected teacher of violin, guitar, mandolin, banjo, flute, clarinet, and saxophone. His wife, Ella, taught piano. The Foggs influenced the lives of many aspiring musicians through their teaching. Fogg also played in Nick Lemmer's Orchestra and composed and published fourteen songs, among which were "Zig Zag Gallop" and "Lily of the Valley Waltz." After he retired, he took up gardening as a means of keeping busy. He was still pursuing this activity vigorously at the age of eighty-eight.

Albert Platte's 1907 composition, "Queen of the Saginaw Valley,"
was written to celebrate Saginaw's fiftieth anniversary as a city.

Albert W. Platte was born in Germany and moved to Saginaw in 1893. He was best known for his work as a classical musician and conductor, and especially as an outstanding teacher in the Saginaw area. Platte ran a two-piano teaching studio in a small building next to his residence on Millard Street. (This small structure later housed some of the facilities of Central Laboratory and, later yet, was moved to the Saginaw River's Ojibway Island, to be displayed, for a few years, as one of Saginaw's historic buildings.) Platte also tried his hand at writing songs, two of which were well known at the time. In 1898, he came up with "Ah, 'Tis a Dream"; and to celebrate the "Saginaw Semi-Centennial" in 1907, he composed "Queen of the Saginaw Valley." The publisher was the Saginaw Printing and Publishing Company.[4]

Saginaw resident John Grinnell Cummings gained widespread recognition for his musical abilities as a composer, organist, choir director, and teacher. He had a formal music background, having studied composition in Berlin with Xavier Scharwenka. One of Cummings's best-known songs was a setting of "In the Gloaming." Another of Cummings's successes was "The Flag of Freedom," written collaboratively with Saginaw lawyer and poet George Grant. At one time, Cummings was elected president of the Michigan Music Teachers' Association. Some accounts hint at a spirited rivalry between Cummings and Platte, but this is difficult to substantiate.

Samuel Richard Gaines, composer, conductor, organist, choirmaster, and teacher, was born in Saginaw. He studied abroad with renowned Czech composer Antonin Dvořák and with several other musicians of considerable stature. After serving the Saginaw area for a number of years, Gaines moved to Boston, where some of his choral compositions won national and international prizes.

John Prindle Scott, who was born in Norwich, New York, spent several years in Saginaw in the very early 1900s. During this time he taught music privately, was the choral music instructor at Saginaw High School, and served as the choir director at the First Presbyterian Church.[5] He com-

---

4. Music publishers of the late 1800s and early 1900s, when not advertising their own publications, often sold advertising space on their sheet music (usually on the back page) much as newspapers and magazines do today. The entire back page of "Queen of the Saginaw Valley" carried such an ad, "Compliments of J. W. Ippel, The Daylight Dry Goods Store of the West Side." The ad featured ladies' embroidered Swiss handkerchiefs for 19 cents, and ladies' long silk gloves for 98 cents a pair.

5. Although it is not the purpose of this book to deal with religious music, the reader may find it interesting to know that the words to the well-known hymn "Stand Up, Stand Up for Jesus" were written by Dr. George Duffield, pastor of Saginaw's First Presbyterian Church from 1869 to 1873.

posed more than seventy songs, many of which were religious. Most of the secular music Scott composed would be categorized as classical; but several of his songs became popular, especially "Good Luck, Mister Fisherman," which he dedicated to some of his friends from Saginaw who accompanied him on fishing trips on the Au Sable River. During one of these trips Scott wrote the words and music to one of his best-known songs, "The Old Road." Another song of interest to Saginaw area residents was Scott's "Riverside Park Reverie," written in recognition of the role this Saginaw River recreational facility played in the lives of many thousands of visitors. Even though many of Scott's songs were written after the Tin Pan Alley era was well under way, his popular music was more reminiscent of an earlier time and would best be termed transitional.

In 1909, two Saginaw residents, Louis E. Hurst (who shoed horses for a living) and Mamie A. Harper, teamed to write what they called a march song, "By the Beautiful Old Saginaw," in honor of the river that flows through the city. The piece is interesting in that its two stanzas are written in strict march time, but the chorus is in 3/4, or waltz time. The song was published by the Catterfield Publishing Company of Saginaw.

The 1912 presidential election motivated two Saginaw residents, Benjamin F. Reed and Mrs. C. P. (Grace) Rieder, to write and publish a campaign song honoring Progressive Bull Moose Party candidate Theodore Roosevelt. The title of the piece was "Hurrah Again for Teddy." In spite of this highly supportive and spirited song, and the fact that Roosevelt carried Michigan, Democrat Woodrow Wilson won the election. (Reed and Rieder may have been related: Rieder's maiden name was Reed.)

Henri W. J. Ruifrok was born in the Netherlands in 1862. He studied music in Europe, taught at several American universities and music conservatories, and finally settled in Saginaw in 1919. By that time, many of Saginaw's songwriters had already developed their musical styles; but Ruifrok exerted a significant influence in the Saginaw area throughout the 1920s as an outstanding teacher at the Saginaw Academy of Music. Additionally, he had written the words and music for a number of songs during the 1890s and 1900s that were characterized by a late Victorian–early Tin Pan Alley transitional style.

Clarence Corbit, a teacher at Arthur Hill High School in Saginaw, wrote "The Assembly March" in 1926. The front page of this march bears

"Hurrah Again for Teddy" was written for the 1912 presidential campaign by Saginaw residents Grace Rieder and Benjamin Reed.

a picture of Arthur Hill High School, then located at the corner of Court and Harrison Streets. The sheet music also includes an arrangement by Corbit of one of Arthur Hill's best-known school songs, "March, March On Down the Field."

Known primarily as a band and orchestra conductor, as a professional trumpet player, and as a music teacher, William (Billy) A. Boos was born in Tiffin, Ohio, in 1865 and moved to Saginaw in 1890. After being very active, musically, in the Saginaw area for about fifteen years, he moved to Detroit, where he played trumpet with the Detroit Symphony Orchestra, directed Detroit's Light Infantry Band, and taught public school music. In 1932, Boos accepted an invitation to return to Saginaw to assume the vacant post of director of the Saginaw Eddy Concert Band. Later, he organized and directed the Saginaw Symphony Orchestra.

Boos was not primarily a songwriter, but several of his compositions, most of which were marches, bear mentioning. He wrote "The United States Secret Service March" in 1942, in honor of his son, who was head of Detroit's Secret Service Office at the time. Boos's "Gay Masquerade," a two-step, made its debut much earlier (1900) at Riverside Park, on the Saginaw River. "The 3275," another march, was given its strange title as a consequence of an unusual incident in Boos's life. Several years earlier, Boos had been serving as a witness in a lawsuit involving two of his fellow musicians as the plaintiff and the defendant. The trial was punctuated by a series of interruptions, many of which were caused by the aging judge, Leander Simoneau, who repeatedly fell asleep on the bench. At one point, the judge recessed the court to watch a parade that happened to be going past the building where the courtroom was located (at the corner of Genesee and Franklin Streets). Finally, when the litigation was finished, Judge Simoneau awarded the plaintiff a $32.75 settlement, thus the name of Boos's song.

Although Boos did not write many songs, he exerted a strong influence over music in the Saginaw area as a conductor, a performer, and a teacher, and he was highly respected by many musicians in the community, both young and old.

Another colorful and significant figure in the Saginaw music scene was Arthur D. Amsden. An extremely capable and versatile alumnus of the New England Conservatory of Music, Amsden was a military band director, a music teacher, an outstanding cornet player, a composer of many cornet solos and songs, and the author of a number of cornet method

"Follow the Band" was written by Arthur Amsden in 1918. The
cover shows Amsden's "running notes" and a picture of
Civil War veterans parading down East Genesee Street.

One of Amsden's later songs, "The Tourist in Florida," was written in 1924.

books, some of which are still printed and in use today. Some of the songs Amsden wrote gained considerable popularity during the early 1900s. Among these were "Pep," "Echo Polka," and "The General Boardman March." A 1918 song by Amsden, "Follow the Band," features on its front cover a photograph of Amsden's band escorting aging Civil War veterans in a parade through downtown Saginaw. Amsden cued in some interesting musical directions to be followed by the pianist and the singer when performing this piece. One such cue exhorts the pianist to imitate "the Lyons (Mich.) Silver Cornet Band." Another calls for the use of a "Kid Tenor" voice, to reach several high notes at the end of the song.

Amsden traveled widely, and wherever he went he made a point of claiming that Saginaw was the one place where "The Star-Spangled Banner" was sung correctly. He also played a major role in establishing the Saginaw Eddy Concert Band, a group that is still heard today, performing at concerts in Saginaw. Although most of Amsden's compositions did not fit in with the Tin Pan Alley style or image, he influenced a remarkable generation of young Saginaw musicians who would leave their mark indelibly on the world of popular music.

Other early Saginaw musicians who helped lay the groundwork for Tin Pan Alley included George Boardman, Joseph Cintura, W. W. Hunt, Felix Jaeger, Mrs. James Jerome, Nellie Mason, W. H. Waghorn, Isaac Wheat, and James H. Norris (who was probably a brother of Charles M. Norris).

Charles K. Harris

3

⊠　⊠　⊠

AFTER THE BALL

UNTIL THE RISE OF TIN PAN ALLEY, most of the popular music in America consisted of marches, formal dance tunes, traditional American folk music, religious music, and occasional melodramatic ballads about death or unrequited love. Such pieces reflected a European influence and the exaggerated discretion and propriety of the Victorian age in the lyrics. The music of Stephen Foster, although enjoyed in some areas, had not yet profited from the benefit of a large, highly organized music publishing industry, and its popularity was comparatively restricted, numerically and geographically. The popular music publishing business had not assumed the key role it was soon to play in mainstream American entertainment, and many of the songwriters and music teachers who were mentioned in the previous chapter were definitely Victorian, or, at least, European in their musical orientation.

Truly national popular American music did not emerge until the late nineteenth century. In 1892 Saginaw's Charles Kassell Harris composed and published "After the Ball," a song still heard today.[1] Eventually it sold more than ten million copies, a fact that was not overlooked by music publishers and other songwriters of the time. After Harris's overwhelming success, it was easy to see that selling sheet music to the rapidly expanding American middle class could be a highly profitable venture. Harris's influence on the popular music scene was solid, diversified, and enduring. A

---

1. Harris's song "After the Ball" was so pre-eminent in the birth and early growth of Tin Pan Alley that author-musician Ian Whitcomb titled his book about the history of Tin Pan Alley *After the Ball.*

This is one of several attractive editions of Harris's "After the Ball."

sign in front of his office in Milwaukee advertised "Songs written to order."
Assessing and responding to public taste would be one of Tin Pan Alley's
major keys to success for decades.

Harris was also instrumental in the actual establishment and subsequent growth of the area that came to be known as Tin Pan Alley. He
used his enormous profits from "After the Ball" to open his own publishing house on West 28th Street in New York City around 1894. This
enterprise was very successful, and soon other music publishers followed
suit and set up shop in this area.

Harris was deeply concerned about protecting the legal rights of songwriters, and he was one of the founding fathers of the American Society
of Composers, Authors, and Publishers (ASCAP). Harris's personal visit
to President Theodore Roosevelt resulted in the enactment of legislation
that determined our present copyright laws.

Harris was born in Poughkeepsie, New York, in 1867. His family moved
to Saginaw when he was still very young. While growing up, he worked
in his father's tailor shop in Saginaw, and later as a bellboy in Saginaw's
Bancroft House hotel. While working in this capacity he came in contact
with many traveling actors and musicians.

During Harris's youth in the city's lumbering era, Saginaw acquired
a reputation as a "live" community where professional entertainers were
certain to find receptive audiences. This reputation lasted for more than a
generation after the lumbering days were over. It was actually enhanced before
the turn of the century when Saginaw made a successful effort to polish up
its image by introducing a number of new cultural enterprises. The result
was a steady stream of professional entertainers passing through town.

One day when Harris was twelve years old, one of the visitors in the
hotel where Harris was working gave him a pass to a performance at the
Saginaw Academy of Music. The next day he informed the man who had
given him the ticket that he had liked the show "better than Buffalo Bill."

After Harris had been introduced to the musical theater in this manner, the impressionable youth made himself a banjo out of an old oyster
can, a broom handle, and some wire. Another traveling musician, hearing young Harris play his homemade musical instrument, was so impressed
by the boy's ingenuity and innate musical ability that he gave Harris an
old banjo of his own. Harris rapidly acquired a high degree of skill on the
instrument, and later, when he hung up his shingle outside his office, it
advertised: "Professor Charles K. Harris, Banjoist and Song Writer."

Harris never learned to read music—he played and composed by ear,
using primarily the black keys on the piano. He would engage the services

of someone who was musically literate (often Joseph Clauder) to transcribe his songs as he created them. His inability to read music led him to become the first songwriter to make use of a moveable piano keyboard, so songs could be transposed readily into singable keys. Some years later, Irving Berlin liked this idea so much that he used it himself. (Throughout the early part of his long career, Berlin also could not read music.)

Harris began composing songs while he was still in his teens, writing both the words and the music. His first published song was "When the Sun Has Set," in 1885.[2] After receiving his first royalty check for this composition (85 cents) he made up his mind that, in the future, he would publish his own music.

In 1892, shortly after leaving Saginaw to set up an office and studio in Milwaukee, Harris took a trip to Chicago. While visiting a dance hall there, he overheard a lovers' quarrel. Using this incident as a musical idea, he composed "After the Ball," which was probably more responsible than any other song for giving birth to the popular music publishing industry, or Tin Pan Alley. The original lyrics for this song portrayed a father telling his daughter about a lost love; but after reflecting on the possible impropriety of such a revelation, Harris decided to alter the lyrics so as to depict a bachelor uncle relating the sad story to a favorite niece, who has asked him why he had never married.

"After the Ball" was first sung in Chicago. The first performance was a failure because the amateur singer who was performing it forgot the words. Undaunted, Harris persuaded a professional singer, James Aldrich Libby, to sing the piece between acts of a matinee at Chicago's Bijou Theater. This time the song was performed in its entirety; and, after a moment of stunned silence at the end of the piece, the audience applauded for five full minutes. It was an enormous hit. Orders for the new song came in so fast that Harris had to borrow funds to get the first 75,000 copies printed. Then the money came in so fast that Harris, whose standard of living had not prepared him for such success, rented safe deposit boxes in which to keep his money.

Interestingly, the Panic of 1893 resulted in a run on a bank near where Harris lived, which happened to be managed by a friend of his. Eager to help, Harris emptied a number of the safe deposit boxes from the bank

---

2. The following six instrumental selections were published by S. Brainard's Sons' Music Publishing House and distributed by C. J. Whitney of Detroit between 1872 and 1892. The authorship of these compositions is attributed to Harris. His first published, documented song appeared in 1885. These may have been early experimental works. If so, these songs would almost certainly have been written in the 1880s: "Belle of the Day," "Mazurka Japonica Waltz," "Princess Amelia Waltz," "Shady Dell Polka," "Sounds from the Plantation" (medley), and "The Three Friends" (medley).

Written by Harris in 1897, "Break the News to Mother" was
popular during the Spanish-American War and World War I.

where he had his cash stored. He then loaded the money on a wagon, drove over to the other bank and conspicuously deposited a sizable portion of his savings there. Other depositors, seeing the huge amount of money Harris was putting into his friend's bank, realized that the bank was unquestionably solvent and stopped withdrawing their money, immediately stopping the bank run.

"After the Ball" became a favorite of John Philip Sousa, who made it a point to have his band perform the number daily at the Chicago World's Fair in 1893. Always the consummate showman (and salesman) Harris embellished the Sousa Band's performances of his song by accompanying them with lantern slide shows. This was the first known use of this combination of entertainment, and it resulted in more copies of the song being sold and more profits for Harris.

By 1900, "After the Ball" had become so deeply ingrained in the hearts of the American public that Harris decided to incorporate a reference to the song in the logo his publishing house printed on every piece of sheet music it sold. In the center of the logo is the inscription "Published by Chas. K. Harris." At the left is a miniature portrait of Harris. At the right is a small cartoon of a round-bellied, spindly-legged, elfin creature chasing a ball half as big as he is. The cartoon bears the obvious caption: "After the Ball."

Another of Harris's highly successful hits was "Break the News to Mother," written in 1897. The title of this song arose from a line in William Gillette's drama, *Secret Service,* in which a wounded drummer boy who has been serving with the army is brought home, meets a servant, and says to him, "Break the news to Mother." Harris had written the line on his shirt cuff the moment he heard it while attending Gillette's play; but it was later, while seated in a barber's chair, that the final idea for the song occurred to him. "I'm going to kill him!" Harris suddenly shouted. He quickly got out of the chair and hurried home to finish the song (probably much to the relief of his startled barber).

The reader may wonder, "Why just break the news to Mother? This young fellow must also have a father: how would Dad be informed?" Harris evidently also thought of this and solved the problem very nicely in the second verse of the song. The act of heroism which had resulted in the drummer boy's mortal wound had been witnessed from across the field of battle by "a noted general," who goes to comfort the dying lad, only to discover the boy is his son, who ran away from home to serve his country. The boy dies in his father's arms, telling him to "break the news to Mother."

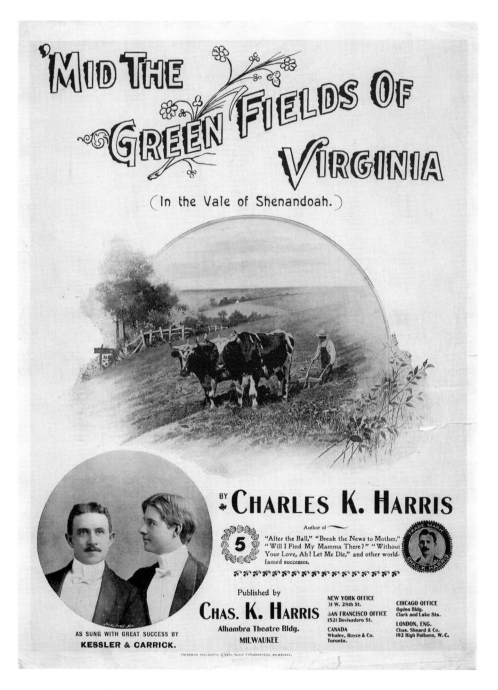

" 'Mid the Green Fields of Virginia," written in 1898, tells
of a young man returning after a long absence to find
that his sweetheart has recently passed away.

This song did not catch on immediately with the public; it had to wait for a war to make it popular. Within a year, an American misunderstanding with Spain proved providential in this respect. The lyrics in the verse refer to "the boys in blue," indicating that Harris set the song in the Civil War, a conflict that was still central to the public consciousness in America. Soon the whole country was singing "Break the News to Mother."

In 1898, Harris published another song that the public quickly took to its liking: "'Mid the Green Fields of Virginia." At that time, Harris had never been anywhere near Virginia, and he freely admitted that he knew absolutely nothing about the state. Nevertheless, the song became extremely popular, selling more than a million copies, and Harris made a handsome profit.[3]

Harris wrote a number of other hits that found great favor with the public. In addition to the three songs already mentioned, his "I'm Trying So Hard to Forget You," "Just Behind the Times," "Always in the Way," "There'll Come a Time," "Would You Care?" "I've a Longing in My Heart for You, Louise," "The Best Thing in Life," and "Better Than Gold" all sold one million, or nearly one million, copies each, which was an amazing volume in those days. This easily earned Harris the recognition of being America's most successful songwriter at the turn of the century.

Another of his biggest hits, "Hello, Central, Give Me Heaven," introduced by a young singer named Al Jolson, tells of a little girl trying to telephone her deceased mother. To read through a list of Harris song titles is to wander through a world of wronged lovers, dying heroes, neglected children, "fallen" women, and relentless moralizing. This was the music that sold at the time, and this was the music in which Harris specialized.

By 1903, Harris had gained worldwide fame as a songwriter. In that year, the famous soprano, Madame Adelina Patti (Baroness Cederstrom), was preparing to make a farewell tour of the United States before returning to her home in Europe. Harris was selected (as a "representative composer") and was commissioned to write a farewell song for Patti to perform at each concert on her tour. The text of the letter Harris received from Patti's agent, Robert Grau, is as follows:

> It is the desire of myself and associates in the farewell tour of Madame Adelina
> Patti to have the famous diva sing an American ballad as an encore. This song

3. Popular music authority Jack Burton, in *The Blue Book of Tin Pan Alley*, writes that Harris's "experience with things Virginian was something less than vicarious. But the abysmal ignorance of a songwriter about his subject does not necessarily prevent him from composing a smash hit on that subject." Jack Burton, *The Blue Book of Tin Pan Alley* (Watkins Glen, N.Y.: Century House, 1962).

Two long-separated lovers are reunited in "For Old Times Sake"
(1900), only to have the young lady die in her fiancé's arms.

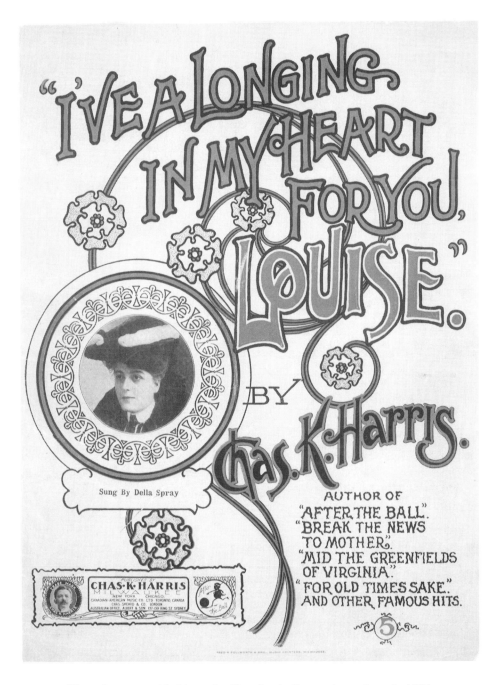

"I've a Longing in My Heart for You, Louise" was also written in 1900.

Composed in 1901, "Hello Central, Give Me Heaven"
was one of Harris's biggest hits.

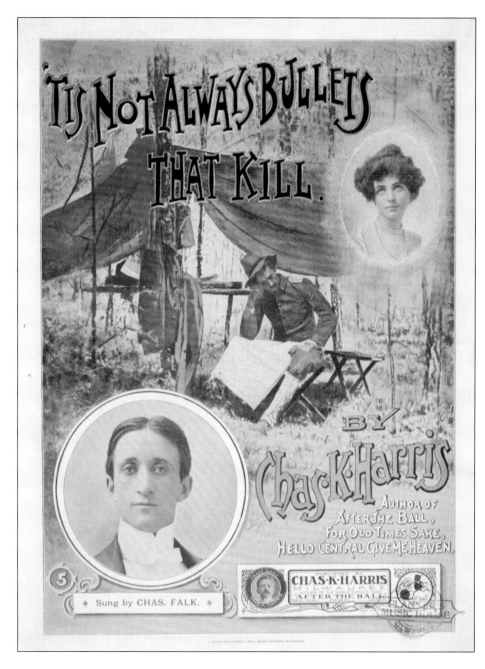

In "'Tis Not Always Bullets That Kill" (1901), a soldier
returning from war admonishes a faithless lover.

This 1903 hit, "For Sale—A Baby," tugged successfully
at the heartstrings of a vulnerable public.

Written in 1910, "It's Always June When You're in Love"
was one of Harris's more optimistic songs.

is to be written by a representative composer and to constitute a work worthy of her artistic endeavors.

I have given much thought as to whom I should commission to write this song and have concluded to tender the offer to you, on the understanding that you are to continue to write and submit your efforts until Madame Patti approves of the selection.

Kindly send me at all times your offerings and I will forward them to the Baroness Cederstrom at her castle in Wales.

Patti approved of Harris's first effort, titled "The Last Farewell," and she performed it at each of her farewell concerts as an appropriate encore. Much to Harris's pleasure (and financial profit) the song was very well received: first by Patti's audiences and later by the general public, which bought more than half a million copies of the sheet music.

In 1914, as World War I was breaking out in Europe, Harris wrote an interesting piece of music, "When Angels Weep." Subtitled "Waltz of Peace," this song begins with obviously religious lyrics, "Glory in the highest, Peace on earth, good will toward men, Glory in the highest," accompanied by a series of high notes on the piano, played as tremolos. Yet, as soon as Harris has succeeded in establishing a reverent mood, he suddenly shifts into a highly energetic Viennese hesitation waltz, which proceeds, mostly without lyrics, for much of the rest of the song. Although a number of Harris's songs had a certain sameness about them, "When Angels Weep" proved that he was no slave to the formal conventions of songwriting. "When Angels Weep" is also among the first songs to reserve special rights. At the bottom of the first page is the statement "Rights for mechanical Instruments reserved." This was a reference to piano rolls and phonograph records.

Harris's music came along at a time when public taste in entertainment was just beginning to go through a change. Harris himself said, years later, "When I began to write songs, we were just emerging from the 'thee and thou' period." He had been told by a traditional music publisher in 1891 that his material could never sell because it had nothing in it about birds and flowers. It was just one year later, with not so much as a word about birds or flowers, that Harris's "After the Ball" became the most popular song America had ever known, or would know for some time.

Harris claimed in 1924 that the demand for some of his "heart story ballad hits," as he called his songs, was as great as ever. But just as his success as a songwriter had ridden in on the crest of a wave of change in public taste, he became increasingly unable to cope with the new tide of syncopated dance rhythms in the popular music which came into style after 1910.[4] His most effective response to this new music was not through any change in the music or the lyrics he wrote, but in the way he advertised his music. Starting about 1911, Harris billed himself as "America's Representative Song Writer," and his sheet music carried a new slogan: "Others strive for ragtime art, Harris reaches for the Heart." By 1915, the public considered Harris's music rather old-fashioned. His "Songs of Yesterday," a piece he published in 1916, demonstrated that even he saw his music as having a nostalgic appeal.

Harris continued to explore possibilities for marketing songs. Musicologist James Geller related how, for the 1924 presidential election, Harris "borrowed" a twenty-year-old march, "Our President," which had been composed by Rudolph Aronson and published by Harris. Harris rewrote the march in three-quarter, or waltz time (imposing some constraints on the piece's effectiveness as a march), added some political lyrics, renamed it "The Calvin Coolidge March to the White House," and attempted to sell it to the Republican Party as a campaign song. The Republicans spurned Harris's proposition, so he altered the lyrics appropriately, and retitled the piece "The John W. Davis March to the White House" (in honor of the Democratic candidate), and sold 100,000 copies of the song to the Democratic Party, which, at the time, was looking for all the help it could get.[5] Coolidge was re-elected, and the "march," which, evidently, had been performed in public only once, quickly and mercifully faded into obscurity, appearing subsequently only on rare occasions as a bizarre footnote in the history of politics and music.

Much to Harris's credit, his music publishing company printed and distributed a good volume of material by many young songwriters, providing them an opportunity to get a start in Tin Pan Alley. One of the best known of these early popular songwriters who benefited from Harris's help was Joseph Howard, writer of "Goodbye, My Lady Love" (1904) and "I Wonder Who's Kissing Her Now" (1909). Harris and Howard joined forces at least once, creating "On a Little Side Street," written in 1921, although by that time both men were well past their songwriting prime.

4. Harris had tried his hand at writing ragtime several years earlier. In 1905, he composed and published a rag called "Back to Life." In *Rags and Ragtime* (New York: Dover, 1978), a musical history by David Jasen and Trebor Tichenor, "Back to Life" is described as "One of the most curious rags ever published. While the form appears typical enough for a Folk rag . . . [and] the tune is fairly orthodox . . . it has the overall effect of a medley, [with very little] holding it together." Jasen and Tichenor also emphasize that the relationship of the keys, or tonalities Harris employs when going from one section of the piece to the next is awkward, at best. Harris apparently was not comfortable composing rags.

5. James Geller, "Mayhem, in Three-Quarter Time," *New Republic* (October 15, 1956).

"Don't Blame Me for Lovin' You" was composed in 1911.

"Will the Roses Bloom in Heaven?" (1911) is asked by an dying child.

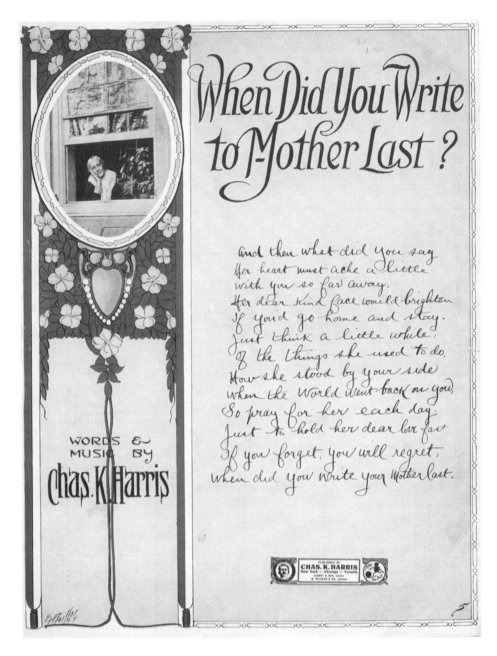

"When Did You Write to Mother Last?" written in 1914,
exhibits Harris's strong emphasis on family values.

Harris composed "Suppose I Met You Face to Face" in 1913.

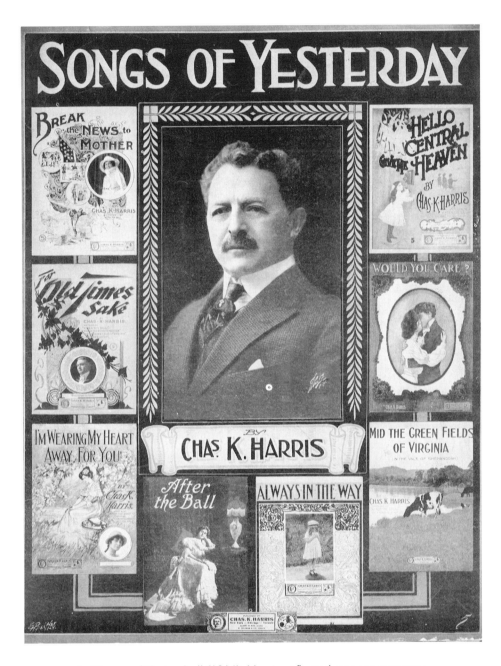

In "Songs of Yesterday" (1916), Harris reflected on past successes.

Harris's "Dancing in a Dream" was probably written in 1930, the year he died. It was quite similar in style to the songs he had written a generation earlier. Harris had grown up in the Victorian era, and even though he had been highly influential in determining a new direction for popular music in America, it was impossible for him to escape entirely the Victorian influence on his music. Times were changing, and so was the nature of American popular music.

4

◩ ◩ ◩

SAGINAW'S EARLIEST ALLEY MEN

Lthough Harris continued writing songs with varying degrees of success for many years, his last important hit was "Always in the Way," published in 1903. Almost twenty years would pass before another songwriter from Saginaw, Isham Jones, would make an impact on Tin Pan Alley that could be compared with Harris's. There were, however, many other popular music composers and lyricists from Saginaw who turned out a wealth of good material that became popular during those two decades. Among the best known of these early Tin Pan Alley men were Arthur McWatters, Joseph Hughes, Fred Cummins, Harry Richardson, James Brockman, Frank Picard, Dan Russo, Carl Rupp, and Olaf "Ole" Olsen.

Arthur J. McWatters was a vaudevillian from Saginaw who had studied music with Louis Toepel and, at one time, had served as a church organist. He wrote both the music and the words to a number of songs in the late 1890s and early 1900s. Among his most popular pieces were "Call Me Darling" and "My Alabama Lady."

In 1899 McWatters composed an interesting waltz called "Hearts or Diamonds." The lyrics tell of a card game between two lovers, in which true love (hearts) triumphs over material wealth (diamonds). Such lyrics were in keeping with the didactic style of the period. The front cover of the song displays two playing cards (queen of hearts and jack of diamonds) as well as a photo of a young man and woman, presumably the couple involved in the card game. The man and woman who posed for the picture were probably McWatters and his wife, fellow vaudevillian Grace Tyson.

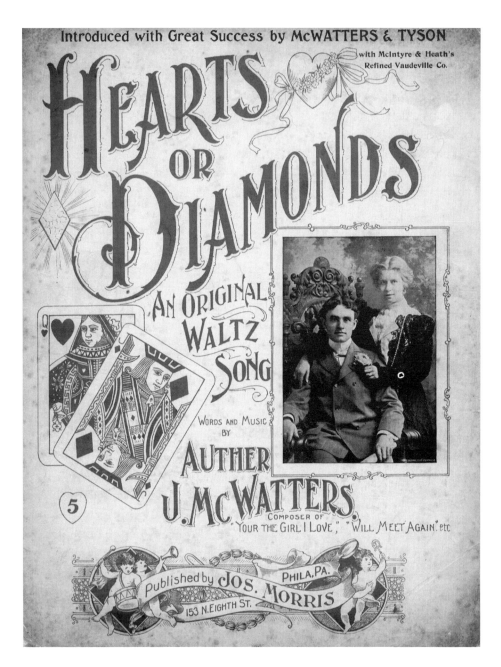

"Hearts or Diamonds" was written in 1899 by vaudevillian
Arthur J. McWatters. Notice the misspelled words.

Also provided on the front cover is the following information about the piece: "Introduced with Great Success by McWatters and Tyson, with McIntyre & Heath's Refined Vaudeville Co." Apparently, McWatters wrote this song with a specific vaudeville act in mind, to be performed by his company. Also of interest is the use of the word "refined" in the company name. Some vaudeville shows in those days based their programs on material that was considered indelicate. McIntyre and Heath wanted the public to know that their shows could be enjoyed by the entire family. Published by Joseph Morris of Philadelphia, "Hearts or Diamonds" was one of the first popular pieces by a songwriter from Saginaw other than Harris to be printed and distributed by a major publishing house.

By the turn of the century, it was becoming increasingly fashionable for middle-class American families to have pianos in their homes. Well aware of this, some major newspaper managers would feature a currently popular song each week as a means of increasing sales. The February 3, 1901 edition of the *New York Journal and Advertiser* carried a piece McWatters had written several months earlier, "Without Thee, Dear Heart."[1] The song bore the inscription, "Written and composed by Arthur McWatters and sung by Miss Mildred Stoller," and displayed a photograph of Stoller.[2]

Saginaw's Joseph H. Hughes, who was an accomplished playwright and actor, wrote several hit songs during the early 1900s. These included "Come into That Dancing Crowd with Me" and "You're My Little Playmate." He also wrote the score for the musical comedy *The Divorce Cure*.

In 1909, Hughes wrote the words and music to a song he dedicated to the Saginaw Wa-was. The Wa-was were a Saginaw rowing team who had excelled in that sport some years earlier, winning many championships between 1870 and 1885. Their colorful name had been derived from an Ojibwe Indian phrase, "Wah-wah-sum," which meant "Lightning-on-the-water." Even though the Wa-was had reached their peak more than a generation earlier, Hughes still felt their achievements warranted commemorating with a spirited song, "Boys of the Winning Team."

The front cover of a song written by Hughes in 1914, "I'm Going Back to That Old Town," features a sketch of a man with his luggage, waiting for a train. A sign, prominently displayed in the station, reads "Saginaw to Detroit, 96 miles."

---

1. Other examples of this practice included the printing of Harris's "Without Your Love, Ah! Let Me Die!" *Chicago American,* January 25, 1903, and his "Belle of the Ball," *Chicago Examiner,* April 14, 1907.

2. Arthur McWatters enjoyed the great outdoors. Even after he moved away from Saginaw in 1904, he returned to the area annually to go duck hunting along the Saginaw and Shiawassee Rivers.

"I'm Going Back to That Old Town" was written in 1914. The
artwork on the cover incorporates a number of creative ideas.

Fred C. Cummins's (sometimes spelled Cummings) regular occupation was that of a drayman. He also collaborated with Joseph Hughes to write the music for Hughes's lyrics to several songs. (Hughes wrote both words and music for some of his popular music.) Among songs written jointly by Hughes and Cummins were "Take a Ride on a Steamboat" and the delightful vaudeville style hit "Would You Like to Take a Walk with Me?"

After Cummins moved away in about 1914, Hughes joined forces with vaudevillian Harry Richardson of Saginaw. Together, they wrote "I'll Anchor My Ship in Your Harbor of Love," "Where the Nightingale Woos the Rose," "The Finest Flag That Flies," and many other songs. "The Finest Flag That Flies" was first written and published in 1914. Two years later, to reflect the American public's growing concern with World War I and growing anti-German feeling, the lyrics to the opening lines of the piece's second verse were completely rewritten. The 1914 version was "There's things I saw so strange to me while I was o'er the sea—Drank beer in dear old Germany." In 1916, the words were changed to "There may be lands across the sea that have their flags so rare, But no flag e'er appealed to me." Old Germany was no longer held as dear.

In 1918, Hughes and Richardson wrote "I'll Come Marching Back to You." The front cover of the song bears an inscription proclaiming that the piece had been "Introduced by Kenneth B. Hughes, The Boy Wonder." It also features a picture of the seven-year-old "Boy Wonder," dressed in a World War I army uniform and carrying a rifle. Joseph Hughes was breaking his son, Kenneth, into show business at an early age. As Kenneth grew older, he became a competent actor, and often was featured in plays with his father.

Hughes and Cummins, and, later, Hughes and Richardson, were Saginaw's first successful songwriting teams, with Hughes generally writing the lyrics. All of the songs written by Hughes, Cummins, and Richardson were published in Saginaw, and many of them were performed by a piano player in Woolworth's store in downtown Saginaw.[3] This was one of the ways popular songs were "plugged," or advertised, for two or three decades.

Although evidence is sketchy, James Brockman probably lived briefly in Saginaw, just after the turn of the century. Understanding that it would hardly be appropriate to claim that his musical tastes and abilities were devel-

---

3. One of my earliest memories, from the mid 1930s, is of accompanying my family as they shopped at Woolworth's. There, the pianist would play one popular song after another, casting a spell on me, which, happily, has lasted to this day.

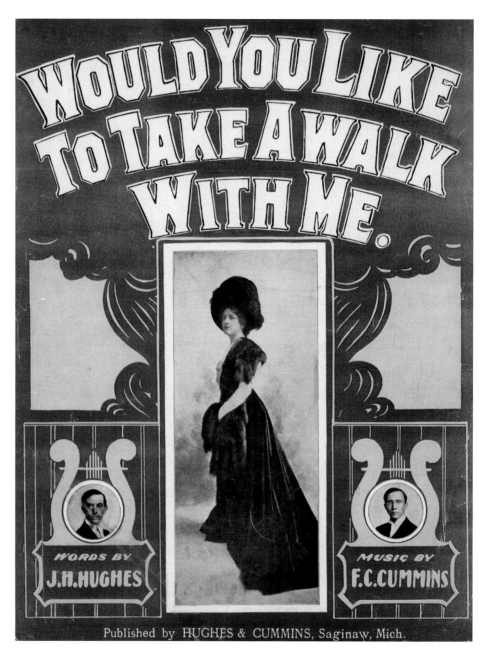

Written by Saginaw's Joseph Hughes and Fred Cummins in
1908, "Would You Like to Take a Walk with Me?" was
written to be performed in vaudeville shows.

Because of World War I, the original 1914 words to
"The Finest Flag That Flies" were changed in 1916.

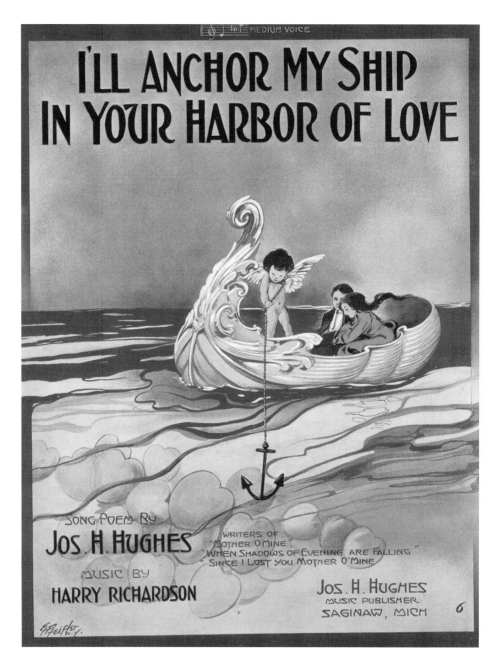

"I'll Anchor My Ship in Your Harbor of Love" was
written in 1915 by Hughes and Richardson.

"Where the Nightingale Woos the Rose" was one
of Hughes's last popular songs, written in 1916.

"Yum Pum Pa," written by James Brockman in 1912, was typical
of the new, energetic popular music that took the place of
the more sedate songs of the 1890s and early 1900s.

oped there to any degree, this talented songwriter still deserves recognition for the many successful songs he wrote, several of which were big hits.

Brockman, who was also an author and a comedian, had some formal training at the Cleveland Conservatory of Music, but his popular songwriting never gave the impression of being weighed down by formal compositional techniques. He wrote the music for some songs, the lyrics for others, and, for a few, he wrote both.

Brockman's most famous hit, "I'm Forever Blowing Bubbles," requires a little explanation. Most publications of this wistful song show it as having been written by Jaan Kenbrovin. This is actually a composite pen name comprised of elements of the names of three men who collaborated in writing this piece: *James Kendis*, *James Brockman*, and *Nat Vincent*.

"I'm Forever Blowing Bubbles," written in 1919, was a deliberate and highly successful effort on the part of its writers to create a theme similar to the previous year's big hit by Harry Carroll and Joseph McCarthy (and Chopin, who actually composed the music but is rarely given credit), "I'm Always Chasing Rainbows."

Brockman wrote many other hits, two of which were extremely successful. His "Feather Your Nest" remained popular throughout the 1920s and well into the 1930s. A song he wrote in 1915, "Down among the Sheltering Palms," was only a moderate success when it first came out, but it enjoyed a spectacular revival in the 1950s. The song was featured in a 1953 film of the same name, starring Mitzi Gaynor, William Lundigan, and Gloria DeHaven. It appeared again in the 1959 movie, "Some Like It Hot." The demand for sheet music and recordings of "Down among the Sheltering Palms" reached an all-time high more than forty years after it had been written.

Some of Brockman's songs were based on humor. His 1908 hit was titled "I Trust My Husband Anywhere, But I Like to Stick Around." The cover page of this song bears the inscription, "Sung with great success by Grace Tyson, of McWatters and Tyson," in *The Motor Girl*, an early musical comedy about how some women were taking to the automobile.

Some of Brockman's other songs, along with their titles, reflected the broken English spoken by people who had recently come to the United States from Europe. One such song, "My Fluff-a de Ruff," also written in 1908, tells about the fluffy ruffles on the Gibson Girl shirtwaist worn by a young Italian immigrant woman. Other such titles used by Brockman were "Hample Pies" (apple pies), "Strumberry" (strawberry), and "Pich" (peach).[4]

4. In the U.S. Immigration Service Museum on Ellis Island, there is a large display of old pieces of popular American sheet music, selected to represent the many nationalities and ethnicities of the people who came to the United States. Among these pieces of music are two by James Brockman, "That's Yiddisha Love," and "Garibaldi," honoring American Jewish and Italian immigrants, respectively.

Brockman's 1915 hit, "Down among the Sheltering Palms,"
was even more popular when it was revived in the 1950s.

"I'm Forever Blowing Bubbles," by Kendis, Brockman,
Vincent, and Kellette, was the biggest hit of 1919.

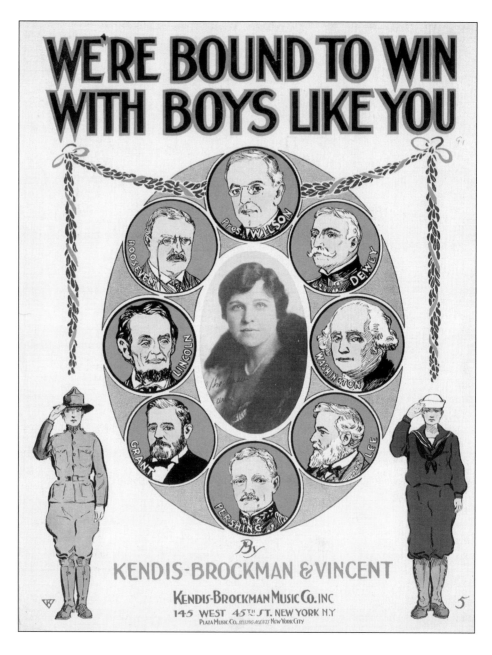

One of Brockman's World War I songs, "We're Bound to Win with Boys Like You," enjoyed moderate success when it was published early in 1918.

Brockman composed "Everybody's Happy Now"
to celebrate the end of World War I in 1918.

Frank A. Picard came from a Saginaw family of ten children. Several of his older brothers, billed as "The Flying Picards," performed as aerialists with major circuses around the country. Frank excelled at anything he attempted. At Saginaw High School, he was quarterback and captain of the football team, and he made a name for himself playing football at the University of Michigan, where he was also an outstanding law student.

After serving in the Army during World War I and rising to the rank of captain, Picard returned to Saginaw to practice law. He soon became involved in politics, and he was so highly regarded that he was nominated by the Democratic Party to run for the lieutenant governor's post in one election and for U.S. senator in another. Although he lost, Picard made a highly creditable showing each time. He served as Michigan's first liquor control commissioner and as Michigan's first commissioner of unemployment compensation. In 1939, President Franklin D. Roosevelt appointed Picard United States Judge of the Federal Court's Eastern Michigan District. He served in this capacity with distinction until his retirement in 1961.

Picard also wrote some popular music early in his career. Besides collaborating with Saginaw songwriter Dan Russo, he wrote both the words and music to a number of other songs, including the entire score to a musical production *Say the Word*, written while he was in the Army.

Picard was a friend of Saginaw songwriter Isham Jones, and they worked together more than once. One song, "C-O-L-U-M-B-U-S," was created by Picard (who wrote the words and music) and was arranged for performance by Jones. Another, "Back to Georgia Bay," was written by Jones and Saginaw lyricist Ole Olsen. Although the lyrics of this piece refer to the state of Georgia, the song's original title was inspired by Picard, whose wife, Ruth, had come from a small Canadian community on the shore of Georgian Bay, Ontario.

Picard's music was very competently conceived: if he had decided to pursue songwriting as a full-time career, he may well have written a number of hit songs.

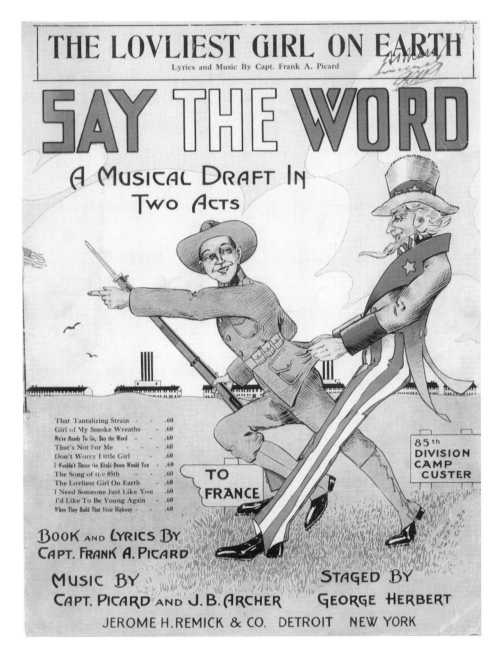

"The Loveliest Girl on Earth" was composed by Frank Picard
in 1918 for the musical stage show *Say the Word*.
Picard's handwritten initials are at the upper right.

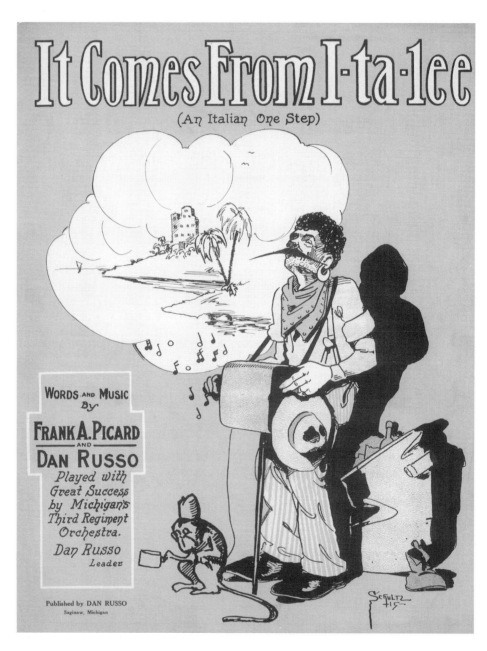

"It Comes from I-ta-lee" was written in 1915 by Frank Picard and Danny Russo.

5

⊡ ⊡ ⊡

FEATURING RUSSO, RUPP, AND OLSEN

ALTHOUGH YOUNG DANNY RUSSO had no desire to become a musician, his father had other ideas. After persuading his son to study the violin, the elder Russo had the boy practice in the back room of the family's fruit market, so he could keep track of his son's musical progress. Whenever Danny hit a sour note, his father would toss a lemon at him. This good-natured criticism evidently helped motivate young Danny. It soon became obvious that he was a precocious learner, as he rose to musical success with surprising speed.

Russo earned his first dollar as a musician at the age of nine. Only a year later, he was good enough to be in demand as a soloist, making his first public appearance in this role with Herman Metz's Band. By the time he was twelve, he was working regularly with some of the area's best dance bands, playing aboard excursion boats that cruised between Saginaw and Point Lookout, about fifty miles to the north. Russo also directed his own band, which played at Saginaw's Bijou, Mecca, and Franklin theaters. By the age of fifteen, he had been named director of Saginaw's prestigious Jeffers Theater Orchestra.

Russo left Saginaw in 1920 and went to Detroit, where, a year later, he organized the Oriole Terrace Orchestra. (Russo said that he chose that name for his group because of his fondness for the sweet voice of the oriole.) Under Russo's leadership, the band produced some outstanding musical figures, including Ted FioRito and Victor Young, each of whom became a highly capable bandleader and songwriter in his own right.

In 1923, the Orioles played at Keith's Palace Theater in Brooklyn, New York, where they were a well received. Subsequently, they enjoyed

Russo's Oriole Terrace Orchestra, as it appeared
in the 1920s. Russo is in center with the violin.

a highly successful engagement at the Arcadia in Detroit, which, in turn, led to a five-year run at Chicago's famous Edgewater Beach Hotel. In Chicago Russo's group established itself as one of the most outstanding jazz dance orchestras in the world, and became the first to broadcast its music over a nationwide radio network (NBC). This musical aggregation recorded many songs on the Brunswick and Columbia labels between 1927 and 1932.

In addition to leading the Orioles, Russo enjoyed a lengthy, distinguished career as a performing musician in the internationally acclaimed bands of Paul Whiteman, Vincent Lopez, and Saginaw's Isham Jones; and he worked extensively in studio bands in Hollywood and elsewhere before retiring in 1947.

Russo's success as a songwriter began in 1915, when he collaborated with lyricist Frank Picard of Saginaw on "It Comes from I-ta-lee." Its lyrics, drawing on Russo's own heritage, told of an Italian immigrant who joyfully sings a melody from the old country as he goes about his business.

By 1915 the United States was going through a period of expansion and prosperity, and Americans were developing a consciousness of feeling good about themselves as a nation. The elements of personal tragedy, so prevalent in the popular music of fifteen to twenty-five years earlier, were being replaced by a new, robust national optimism.

Russo also was involved in the 1921 musical comedy *Bombo,* which focuses on a ship's deckhand who helps Columbus discover America. It is easy to understand why Al Jolson, who starred in the production, kept

Russo undoubtedly had a much more rustic setting in mind than today's Hackensack offers when he wrote "Back in Hackensack New Jersey" in 1924.

inserting new songs into the show to divert the audience's attention from the less-than-fascinating plot. Russo and Ted FioRito composed the music to the best-remembered song from *Bombo*, "Toot, Toot, Tootsie, Goo'Bye." The words to this great hit were written by one of Tin Pan Alley's most famous lyricists, Gus Kahn. "Toot, Toot, Tootsie, Goo'Bye" was an instant success, and it remained popular for many years. This song was sung again by Jolson in the 1927 Academy Award–winning motion picture *The Jazz Singer*. This film was historic because it was the first well-

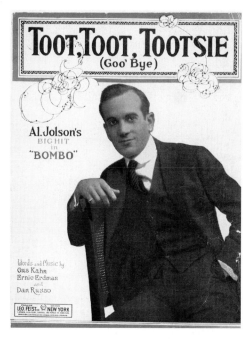

known "talking picture." In 1946, "Toot, Toot, Tootsie, Goo'Bye" enjoyed another sensational revival, and it is still heard from time to time.

Altogether, Russo wrote, or helped write, thirty-two songs. In addition to those already mentioned, his compositions include "I Couldn't Help It if I Tried," "California Rose," and the beautiful hit song "Roses."

In some respects, the early musical career of Saginaw's Carl Rupp was similar to that of Russo. As a boy, Rupp preferred playing baseball to playing the piano, but his father, who was a church organist, did not lose hope that his son would make music an important part of his life. Eventually the boy developed a great interest in music. Once he became serious about learning to play, Rupp's progress was so rapid that by the age of fourteen, he, like his father, also had been appointed as a regular church organist—at St. Paul's Episcopal Church, in Saginaw. After attending Saginaw High School for two years, Rupp worked as a window trimmer in several stores in downtown Saginaw, including Wiechmann's Department Store. He remained very involved in music during this time, however, and by 1917, he was traveling with his own band.

In 1923, the Carl Rupp Dance Orchestra became one of the first to be heard over the air, through the facilities of radio station WTAM, in Cleveland, Ohio. Rupp and his orchestra continued to enjoy popularity in radio broadcasting for more than ten years, after which Rupp was named musical director of radio station WJAY in Cleveland.

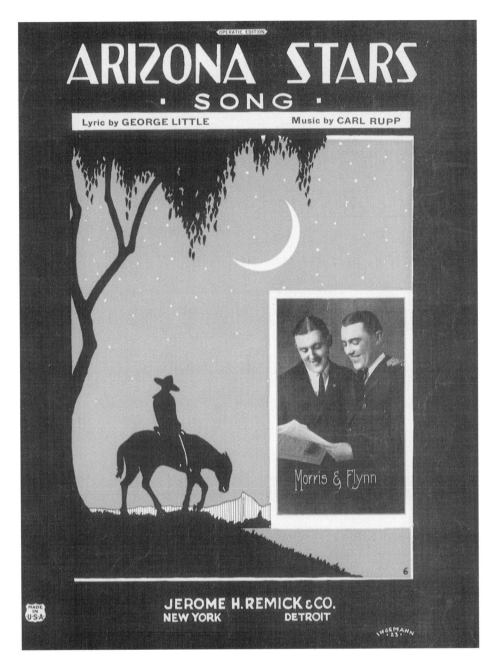

"Arizona Stars" (1923) was one of Carl Rupp's earliest successes.

Rupp's "Footloose," written in 1925, was one of the most popular dance tunes of the 1920s. (Used by permission, Sam Fox Publishing Company.)

The Original "**Footloose**" Strut

Dance Sensation of the Year

BY

NED WAYBURN

IN SLIDE STEPS, PLACE. RIGHT FOOT FIRST—THEN DRAW LEFT TO IT.

HOW TO DANCE IT

THIS dance is so simple and fits the rhythm of the music so perfectly that you scarcely need any instruction other than the movement of the feet as shown in the diagram of the dance

Count the complete dance in four sets of five counts each. First you count "ONE, two," then more quickly "One two three."

The counts shown on the diagram and these numbers correspond to the description of each step as follows.

A—First step out with the left foot. (1)

B—Step forward a full step with the right foot. (2)

Now take three short steps, more quickly, which are:

C—Forward with the left. (1)

D—Forward with the right. (2)

E—Forward with the left. (3)

F—Step the right foot out to the right and on the same count quickly glide the left foot to the right one. (1)

G—Repeat, the right foot again to the right and glide the left to it. (2)

H—With the right foot step out forward and to the right, also turning the foot a little to the right. (1)

I—Step with the left foot forward and turning the body a little to the right. (2)

J—Step backward with the right foot, this step completing a quarter turn of the body. (3)

K—Step back with the left. (1)

L—Step back with the right. (2)

Now take three short steps backward which are:

M—Step back with the left. (1)

N—Step back with the right. (2)

O—Step back with the left. (3)

P—Step out to side with the right foot and on the same count slide the left foot to the right. (1)

Q—Again step out to the side with the right foot and slide left to it. (2)

R—Step forward and to the right with the right foot, turning to the right. (1)

S—Step with the left foot, circling it across and in front of the right foot, and turn to the right, pivoting on the ball of the right foot. (2)

T—Complete the turn of the body, pivoting on the ball of the left foot as you step backward with the right, swinging it as you turn. (3)

Back cover of "Footloose." Some dance hits of this period featured instructional diagrams such as this on the back covers of the music. (Used by permission, Sam Fox Publishing Company.)

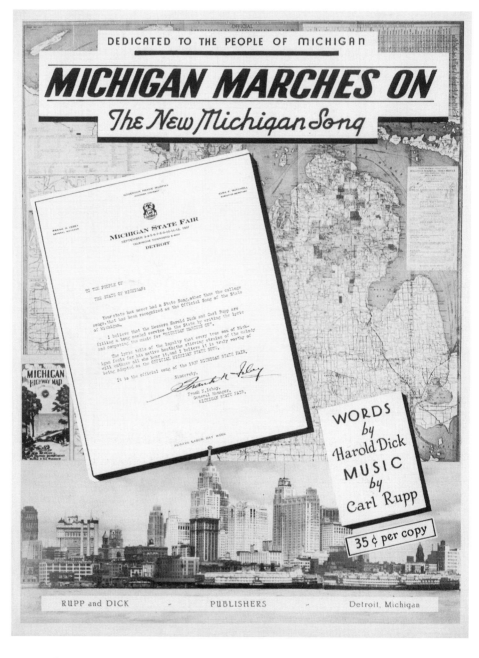

Rupp tried, unsuccessfully, to have "Michigan Marches On" adopted as
Michigan's official state song. Notice the Detroit skyline,
as it appeared in 1937.

Although Rupp's formal education was limited, he was a very bright individual. One of his more interesting accomplishments was his invention of an electrical device that simplified the teaching of piano.

Between 1920 and 1940 Rupp wrote many popular songs, several of which became big hits. "My Sweetie and Me" and "The Flapper Wife" were both popular in the mid 1920s, and "My Sweetie and Me" enjoyed a highly successful revival in 1950. Rupp's "Footloose," which came out in 1925, was one of the big dance tunes of the late 1920s and remained popular into the 1930s. The back cover of the sheet music for "Footloose" is entirely devoted to explaining how to dance "The Original Footloose Strut." The explanation is accompanied by intricate diagrams, illustrating precisely how the feet should be moved. The first page of this song bears an advertising message used occasionally during this period: "Get this song for your player piano or talking machine." In 1937, working with lyricist Harold Dick, Rupp wrote and published "Michigan Marches On," hoping the piece would be adopted as the official state song. Although disappointed that the idea failed to gain the necessary support, Rupp continued his career as a successful writer of popular songs.

Olaf Werner Olsen, who became known as "Ole" Olsen, started taking classical piano lessons when he was about six years old, but he soon developed a strong preference for other kinds of music. Within a few years he was playing in dance bands in the Saginaw area. When Olsen was thirteen and fourteen he spent his summers in Chicago, living with his uncle and playing piano in local beer gardens there. Another summer he played with Arthur Amsden's 33rd Regimental Band. These experiences gave Olsen a taste for excitement and travel and by the time he was in his early twenties he had gone to Chicago to write songs and to play in Isham Jones's band.

Although Olsen wrote both the words and the music to some songs, he earned much of his recognition by writing the lyrics to such early Isham Jones hits as "Frisco's Chinatown," "That's Jaz," and the popular World War I songs, "There's One More River We're Going to Cross and That's the River Rhine" and "We're in the Army Now." (The latter should not be confused with Irving Berlin's "You're in the Army Now.")

Olsen was not a typical lyricist: the words he wrote frequently centered around some unconventional topic or humorous story. Two excellent examples of this are his lyrics for "Oh! Min!" and "Call for Mr. Brown." "Oh! Min!" focuses on amusing incidents in Sidney Smith's engaging comic strip of years gone by, "Andy Gump." "Call for Mr. Brown" deals with a

"Cremona Man" was written in 1916 by
Saginaw's Olaf "Ole" Olsen and Isham Jones.

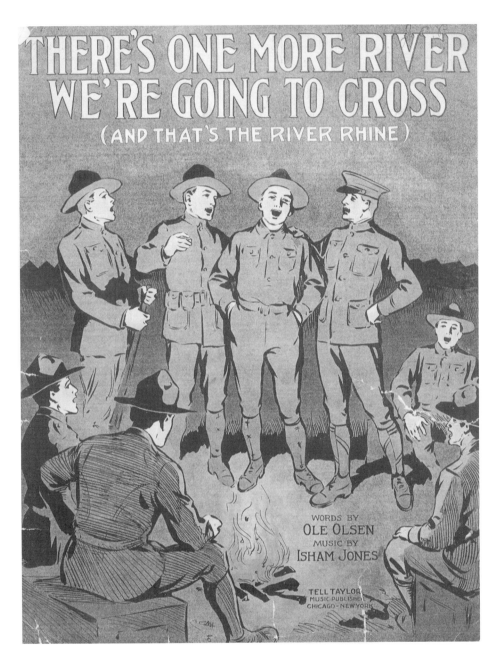

"There's One More River We're Going to Cross"
(1918) was a World War I hit by Olsen and Jones.

Based on ideas from a comic strip, Olsen
and Jones composed "Oh! Min!" in 1918.

Another humorous song by Jones and Olsen, also
written in 1918, was "Call for Mr. Brown."

thoroughly frustrated bellboy who dreads paging a certain Mr. Brown, because he never can be found.

Olsen earned the distinction of having been one of the very few song-writers to have had pieces published about both world wars. One of his last known songs was "When Will the War Be Over?" written in 1943.

Several of the songs written jointly by Olsen and Jones were published by the Michigan Music Publishing Company of Saginaw. The publisher's slogan, printed at the bottom of the front cover of each piece of sheet music was "Songs with a Kick." The slogan was accompanied by a logo that sometimes featured a bucking mule, and sometimes a high-stepping can-can dancer.

After Olsen and Jones decided, amicably, to go their separate ways, Olsen concentrated on organizing and leading his own dance band. Singer Eva Tangway, the famous "I Don't Care Girl" of the 1920s, heard Olsen and his band and liked their style of playing so much that she engaged them to accompany all of her performances for two years.

Another accomplishment of Ole Olsen's band was that, like Carl Rupp's band, it was one of the first to be heard over the air—in the Olsen Band's case, over radio station WIP in Philadelphia.

6

⊠　⊠　⊠

IT HAD TO BE JONES — WONDERFUL JONES!

WHEN, AT THE AGE OF TWELVE, Isham Jones composed "Mid-summer Evenings," few probably suspected that this song was the first published effort of an emerging giant of Tin Pan Alley. Born in Coalton, Ohio, in 1894, Jones moved to Saginaw with his family when he was still a young boy. His father was a miner; and by the time young Jones had reached his teenage years, he, too, was employed at a mine near Saginaw, driving a mule and a string of coal cars. Music, however, was the real driving force in his life. Jones had his first engagement as a professional musician at age eleven, playing guitar at the Mead Dance Hall, just west of Saginaw. Later, he also became proficient on the violin, cello, and piano, and he acquired an exceptional level of expertise on saxophone.

Jones got his first big break in music at age seventeen while attending a musical at Saginaw's old Jeffers-Strand Theater. The pianist in the orchestra suffered a stroke and had to be carried from the theater. Jones jumped into the orchestra pit, started playing piano with the orchestra, and the show went on, flawlessly. The contacts he made from this unscheduled performance eventually led to Jones's rise to international prominence--as an outstanding performer, arranger, and bandleader, and as a songwriter of immense talent.

After leading the popular Rainbow Gardens Orchestra on Chicago's south side before he was twenty-one years old, Jones formed his own band. The Isham Jones Band was known as a musicians' band, distinguished by the high level of musicianship demanded by Jones and exhibited consistently by its members. The superb performing ability of the musicians who played in Jones's band was exploited to the fullest by the musical arrange-

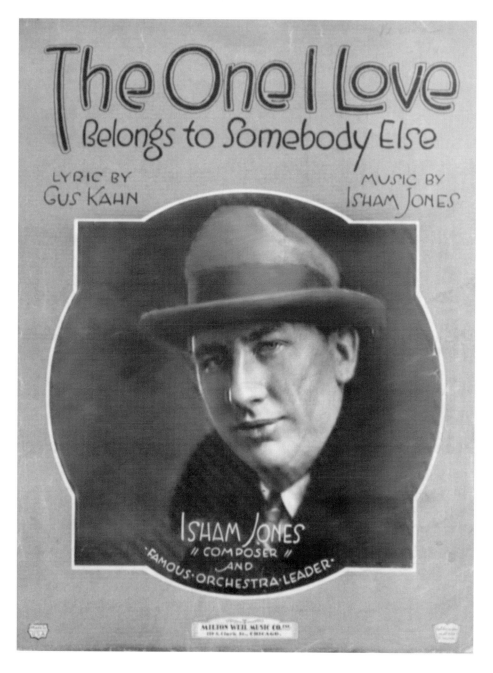

The cover of his 1924 hit, "The One I Love Belongs to Somebody Else," features a portrait of the gifted Isham Jones.

ments Jones himself conceived. His arrangements employed a remarkable variety of creative technical devices and instrumentation. In his book *The Swing Era,* Gunther Schuller says that, along with Paul Whiteman and Art Hickman, Isham Jones was "one of the three prime innovators in determining the basic instrumentation and character of the modern American dance band."[1]

The sound of the Jones Band was so admired by other top bandleaders of the late 1920s and 1930s that many attempted to pattern their own arrangements after those created by Jones. Notable among these bandleaders were Swing Era greats Gene Krupa and Lionel Hampton. The Isham Jones Band was so successful that, along with Paul Whiteman's Dance Band, it was considered the best in the world at the time, with Jones playing in Chicago and Whiteman in New York. (At this time Saginaw's Dan Russo was directing what was generally accepted to be the best dance band between New York and Chicago: the Oriole Terrace Dance Orchestra in Detroit.)

By 1925, the Isham Jones Band's phenomenal success had led to an extended engagement at the elegant Kit Kat Club in London, England, where some of the musicians who worked for Jones were paid $450 a week. This was an unheard-of salary for sidemen, and at that time it made them the highest paid in the world.

The Isham Jones Band was in constant demand and, among many other engagements, it was selected to be the featured instrumental group for the Miss America Pageant of 1927.[2] Jones found it virtually impossible to keep up with the requests for his musical talents. On one occasion, he attempted to refuse an unwanted offer to direct a theater orchestra by asking for the outrageous salary of $3,000 a week for the part-time position. His ploy failed, however: the $3,000 figure was instantly accepted and he was immediately handed a contract. Jones changed his mind and took the job.

The Isham Jones Band owed a good part of its success to Jones's awareness of public taste, and he was uniquely equipped with all the means of responding to it sensitively. Moreover, he was so creative that, at times, he actually played a role in reshaping, and even elevating, public taste—a feat accomplished by very few.

When Hoagy Carmichael wrote "Stardust" in 1929, he originally composed the song for piano only, with no lyrics, to be played at a faster tempo

---

1. Gunther Schuller, *The Swing Era* (New York: Oxford University Press, 1989).

2. Isham Jones was not the only individual from Saginaw to be directly involved in the 1927 Miss America Pageant. Miss Saginaw, twenty-year-old Charlotte Bowman (later to become Mrs. Roy Benway), was one of one hundred contestants in the pageant.

than we are accustomed to hearing it—almost in a ragtime style. It was later presented to the public through a recording by the Isham Jones Band, arranged by Jones, and played, for the first time, as a slow ballad. After hearing the Jones arrangement of "Stardust," lyricist Mitchell Parish put some beautiful words to it, resulting in what many consider the greatest popular song ever written.

Whenever Jones's other responsibilities prevented him from having enough time to write arrangements for his band, he saw to it that this important task was left in only the most capable hands. The arrangers whose services he engaged included Les Brown, Gordon Jenkins, and Fletcher Henderson, who were, along with Jones, probably the best in the world at that time.

The Isham Jones Band flourished for a number of years, both in public performances and as a recording ensemble. Between 1920 and 1927, they recorded more than two hundred songs. A perfectionist, Jones continued to insist on hiring only the best musicians in the business; and when, because of poor health, he stepped down as leader in 1936, the band was taken over by one of its members: an up-and-coming clarinet and saxophone player named Woody Herman.

Herman enjoyed relating an incident that occurred during one of the engagements. Jones, who always read from the music as he directed the band, was using a large wooden box to hold his music. Herman hid in the box and, in the middle of a song, stuck his hand out through a small opening in the top of the box and waved it in Jones's face. As soon as Jones recovered from being "scared out of the park," as Herman described it, he chased Herman off the bandstand.

Although Jones's first composition was published in 1906, he did not begin writing songs on a regular basis until about 1912. By the time he was twenty, in 1914, half a dozen of his songs had been published. Between 1916 and 1918, he teamed with Saginaw's Ole Olsen to write many more songs, several of which became popular. About this time Jones was in a serious accident in Saginaw. A car in which he was a passenger was hit by a train, killing one of the car's occupants and injuring Jones and the others. This incident left him depressed for some time, and it may have played a part in his decision to leave Saginaw and move to Chicago. There, Jones was able to get a job on the composing staff of the Waterson, Berlin, and Snyder Publishing House. Irving Berlin headed the firm's composing department and recognized Jones's tremendous potential.

Soon Jones was turning out one outstanding song after another. His creativity was virtually limitless. On the few occasions when he borrowed

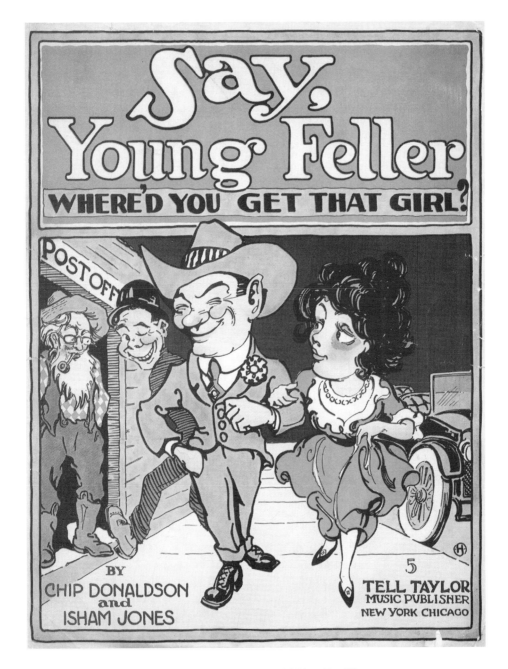

"Say, Young Feller, Where'd You Get That
Girl?" was written by Jones in 1918.

Jones wrote "What'll You Do?" in 1921.

thematic material from others for his compositions, he displayed excellent taste in the material he selected, and he employed extraordinary originality in the way he treated it. Two examples of this, both probably written in 1922, were "Pilgrim's Blues," a dance band arrangement of "The Pilgrim's Chorus," from Wagner's opera *Tannhauser,* and "Samson and Delilah," an arrangement of "My Heart at Thy Sweet Voice," from Saint-Saens's opera *Samson and Delilah.*

By 1924, Jones was recognized as a great songwriter by both his colleagues and the public. In that year alone, he composed four songs that are still considered all-time hits. By then Jones and his band were playing a long-term engagement in Chicago. As he walked to work from his nearby north side apartment, he regularly passed a music store window displaying a piano he greatly admired but could not bring himself to buy. His wife found out about the piano, secretly purchased it, and gave it to him as a surprise gift for his thirtieth birthday. That night, it is said that Jones sat at his new piano for hours composing, inspired by the splendid sound of the instrument. By morning, he had composed three of his best-known hits: "It Had to Be You," "Spain," and "The One I Love Belongs to Somebody Else."

Saginaw trombonist Paul Daines recalls another example of Jones's creative genius. One evening in 1930, during an intermission at a dance where his band was playing, Jones came up with a musical idea. Before the brief intermission was over, he had composed an entire song, which soon became popular: "What's the Use?"

Many Isham Jones songs have been featured in movies. "It Had to Be You" was prominently highlighted in the 1944 film, "Show Business," starring Eddie Cantor and George Murphy. This resulted in heavy demands for sheet music and recordings of the song. Republishing the sheet music presented no problem, but because many performing musicians were in the armed services at that time, the musicians' union, under the leadership of James Caesar Petrillo, had declared a ban on making any new recordings. RCA Records, however, found a way to circumvent the moratorium by reissuing an Earl "Fatha" Hines recording of "It Had to Be You," which had originally been pressed and distributed in 1941. The song immediately became a best seller again, in terms of both record and sheet music sales. In 1956, "It Had to Be You" was featured in a movie of the same name, which starred Ginger Rogers and Cornell Wilde. Again, record and sheet music sales soared, and, for the third time, this song became a hit. As recently as 1989, "It Had to Be You" became popular again after it was featured in the film "When Harry Met Sally."

Jones's first big hit was "On the Alamo," composed in 1922.

One of the best-loved songs of the entire Tin Pan Alley era,
"I'll See You in My Dreams" was written by Jones in 1924.

Jones composed "What's the Use?" in 1930 during an
intermission at a dance where his band was performing.

In popular American dance music, every generation has had its own "good night song," a well-known tune that signals the end of the evening. Jones's "I'll See You in My Dreams," written in 1924, has served two, or even three generations in this capacity, and the song is still popular after more than sixty years. This nostalgic piece also enjoyed a revival in the movie "Show Business," and again, in the 1951 film about the life of Jones's most famous songwriting partner, lyricist Gus Kahn, appropriately titled "I'll See You in My Dreams." "It Had to Be You" and "I'll See You in My Dreams" have been featured in no less than forty feature-length films.

Popular music by Saginaw songwriters can be heard in many motion pictures. The film "I'll See You in My Dreams" features five of these songs. In addition to the title song and "It Had to Be You," two more of Jones's hits appear: "Swingin' down the Lane" and "The One I Love Belongs to Somebody Else." Russo's immortal "Toot, Toot, Tootsie, Goo'Bye" is also included in this movie.

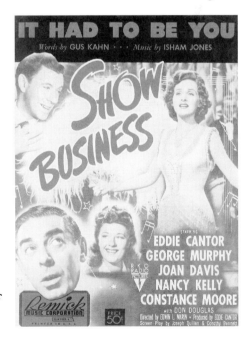

Jones ran his own publishing company for a brief period during the mid 1930s. Some of the sheet music printed by the Isham Jones Music Corporation featured on its back cover a four-inch high portrait of Jones, accompanied by the following message: "You have just played a song carefully selected for your approval by Isham Jones, Internationally famous Composer and Orchestra Leader." These words were followed by a list of about ten of Jones's best-known hits. As with

advertising by other songwriters, modesty did not appear to fit in with Jones's plan for marketing his music.

Just as Harris had done with his publishing company years before, Jones provided an opportunity for other songwriters to get their music before the public. For example, Jones published at least two songs by Saginaw's Gerald Marks. Although his publishing business was moderately successful, Jones felt that the demands it imposed on him took too much time away from his first love: the music itself. So, after a year or two, he decided to leave publishing to others and devote himself fully to composing, arranging, and leading his band.

7

▨　▨　▨

LORENZO'S LULLABY FOR A LOVELY LADY

ONE SUMMER EVENING IN 1955, I was playing in a band at the Argonne Night Club, near Charlevoix. Our group had just finished performing a song we thought we had interpreted quite well, and we were taking a moment to congratulate ourselves on what a wonderful job we felt we had done. At that point, an elderly gentleman walked up to the bandstand and informed us that he knew more about the piece we had just played than we did.

Needless to say, we were less than ecstatic to hear this, but we decided to listen to this man. There was something about his manner, perhaps the quiet authority in his voice, that intrigued us. We soon learned that it was, indeed, worth our while to pause and hear what he had to tell us. He was Angelo "Ange" Lorenzo, who lived in Saginaw, and the song we had just played was "Sleepy Time Gal," which he had written in 1923. For the only time in the band's history, we discarded our firm policy of never playing the same song twice in a row; and, after introducing our guest, we played "Sleepy Time Gal" again, this time with Lorenzo at the piano. We had always enjoyed the piece, but had never before fully appreciated just how good a song it was until hearing it played by the man who had written it.

Lorenzo was born in West Branch and did not move to Saginaw until about 1940. Unlike most of the songwriters discussed here, Lorenzo's early musical interests and abilities developed elsewhere. Nevertheless, he frequently came into contact with a number of the songwriters who did grow up in Saginaw, and it can be assumed that exchanges of musical ideas often occurred. Also, after moving to Saginaw, Lorenzo teamed with Howard "Howdy" Quicksell to write a number of songs.

"Aladdin's Bungalow," written by Ange Lorenzo in 1916, was
actually a singing commercial, advertising prefabricated homes.

In the early 1920s, Ange Lorenzo had formed an eight-piece dance band called the Tunesters, which played at the Detroit Athletic Club through-out most of the year and at Juilleret's Cabaret (a fashionable Harbor Springs resort for wealthy vacationers) during the summer months. The Tunesters and their friends wore white flannel trousers and blue jackets, or short skirts and rolled stockings, and they drove Stutz Bearcats or Jordan Play-boy Roadsters. Coonskin coats, hip flasks, and cars with running boards and rumble seats were in style with the crowd at Juilleret's. The song "Sleepy Time Gal" was born during this "Roaring Twenties" milieu.

On a summer morning in 1923, while seated in the dining room at Juilleret's, a friend of Lorenzo's (amateur songwriter Joseph Alden, from Grand Rapids) showed Lorenzo some lyrics he had written, along with the title "Sleepy Time Girl." Lorenzo took the lyrics, walked over to the piano and sat down, an idea forming in his mind. "The notes just fell into place almost perfectly the first time we went through it," Lorenzo said, recalling the incident years later. "The theme was there in that first play-ing. It was a natural . . . one of those one-in-a- million things." That night the Tunesters introduced the song to the patrons of Juilleret's. It was an instant hit—the crowd loved it.

Lorenzo and Alden tried for some time to get "Sleepy Time Girl" before the American public, but the geographical and numerical scope of their audience was limited. Then, in 1925, the famous songwriting team of composer Richard Whiting and lyricist Ray Egan heard the song and recognized its potential. Employing their considerable talents, they pol-ished up the song's lyrics a little, renamed it "Sleepy Time Gal," and had it published.

The piece was an immediate hit, and remained a favorite for more than a generation. It became so well known that in 1953, thirty years after it was written, Lorenzo received a letter addressed simply to "Ange Lorenzo, Sleepy Time Gal, Saginaw, Mich." Musicians still refer admiringly to this piece as an "evergreen"—a song whose lyrics and music possess a time-less universal appeal to audiences and musicians alike.

Other songs by Lorenzo include "Sweet Forget-Me-Not," "Rainy Days," and "Watching for Your Shadow." One of his early efforts, "Aladdin's Bungalow," was commissioned in 1916 by Aladdin Prefabricated Homes, of Bay City. Actually a rhyming advertisement consisting of two verses and two choruses, Lorenzo's lyrics urge the listener, "If it storms, if it blows, if it rains, or it snows, Get an Aladdin." The music Lorenzo provided for this piece (which attained some popularity) is a well-written example of pre-1920 ragtime. Another song by Lorenzo, written in collaboration with

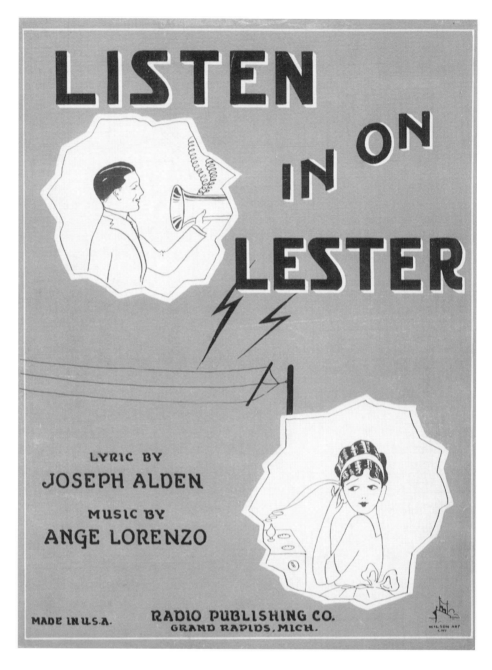

Lorenzo composed "Listen in on Lester," a
humorous song about a ladies' man, in 1922.

One of the truly great hits of Tin Pan Alley, "Sleepy Time Girl," written
by Lorenzo in 1923, did not catch on with the public until the
title was changed to "Sleepy Time Gal" in 1925.

Joseph Alden, was "Listen in on Lester," a piece about a fellow who bears constant watching because of his tireless zeal for developing friendly relationships with the ladies.

After spending many successful years as a pianist for several publishing houses and for various dance bands, Lorenzo moved to Saginaw to own and operate the Daniel Theater. He continued to compose, writing some songs by himself, and some in collaboration with Howdy Quicksell. The best known of these combined efforts was "I Want the Girl of my Dreams to Be the Girl in My Arms." There were more songs by Ange Lorenzo, many of them good, but none ever achieved the lasting popularity of his delightful little lady from the 1920s. Many have attempted to describe "Sleepy Time Gal." Lorenzo himself probably said it best: "I like to think there was such a person and imagine she was a real beauty—and certainly a lady. One who never got old."

Ange Lorenzo died in 1971, at the age of seventy-seven. At the funeral, his long-time friend, Saginaw musician Bill Kempf, played and sang a final tribute to Lorenzo, "Sleepy Time Gal."

8

❖ ❖ ❖

SAGINAW GETS THE BEST MARKS IN MUSIC

At the age of thirteen, Gerald Marks of Saginaw sent a piece of music he had written, along with the following letter, to songwriter Irving Berlin. "I am enclosing my latest song. After looking it over, I know that you will come to the conclusion that I am loaded with talent. You and I could make a lot of money together. Let me hear from you. Yours truly, Gerald Marks." Many years later, Berlin and Marks would share a laugh over this.

As a young man, Gerald Marks played piano for vaudeville acts at the Jeffers-Strand Theater, and in dance bands at Riverside Park, near Saginaw. He also worked for a time as a stenographer for the Saginaw Standard Oil Company, but he fell asleep while taking dictation and was encouraged to seek employment elsewhere. It eventually became obvious to everyone, including Marks himself, that he belonged in the music business.

After a few years of playing in bands around the Saginaw area, Marks moved to Detroit, where he found work playing piano with a band there. In 1926, the leader of this band fell victim to a lengthy illness and Marks took over as leader. The group flourished under his direction. One of the members of this band was a saxophone player named Glen "Spike" Knoblauch. Some time later, Knoblauch changed his name to Glen Gray, and formed his own group: the famous Casa Loma Orchestra (named after a Toronto nightclub, which failed to open).

At about this time Marks seriously began pursuing songwriting as a career. Three of his early efforts became fairly well known in the late 1920s: "Everybody Has Someone But Me," "As Long As I Live," and the lovely "I'd Walk a Million Miles to Be a Little Bit Nearer to You." Then, in 1931,

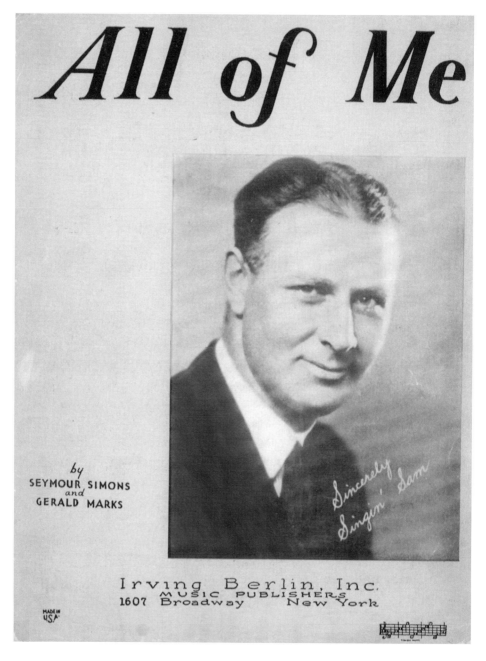

"All of Me" became one of the biggest hits in the history of Tin Pan
Alley. (Used by permission, Bourne Company Music Publishers.)

Marks, working with Detroit lyricist Seymour Simons, wrote a song that achieved such lasting popularity that it is still considered a standard today: "All of Me."

Initially, Marks and Simons had trouble marketing "All of Me." In Marks's words, "Every song publisher in New York turned the song down."[1] Disappointed, but knowing he had a good song to get before the public, he took "All of Me" to Belle Baker, who was, at the time, the featured singer at Detroit's Fisher Theater. Baker, who had established a commendable reputation as an entertainer, first in vaudeville, and then in radio, was deeply moved by the song, especially the line "Your good-bye left me with eyes that cry," which reminded her of her husband, who had recently passed away. She agreed to sing the song as part of a radio broadcast she would be making soon from New York City. Two weeks later, her voice filled with emotion, Baker sang "All of Me" over the radio. The next day, music stores and song publishers were swamped with requests for the song—Marks and Simons had an instant hit.

One of Marks's favorite anecdotes centered around his visit to the home of sultry movie star Mae West, to ask her to record "All of Me," once the song had become a hit. West invited Marks in, showed him to her piano, and told him in her smolderingly seductive voice, "Do it for me, Gerald," meaning, of course, for him to play "All of Me" for her. "So I sat down at the piano and I did it for her," Marks said. "You had to be made of iron to withstand what I withstood. She sat at the piano right there—and about ten or twelve feet in back of her, stood a three-quarters size nude statue of her. So, in your line of vision, you could have either Mae West dressed or Mae West undressed. It's a good thing that I know that song mechanically; otherwise, I'd have gotten all mixed up in the words, I'm sure." West liked the song and recorded it.[2]

In 1935, Marks came up with another big hit, "That's What I Want for Christmas," sung by Shirley Temple in the movie *Stowaway*. The next year, working with lyricist Irving Caesar, Marks composed a song he was certain would be another great success: "The Rooster's Crowin'." Hoping to get this song before the public, he sent a copy of it to singer Al Jolson, encouraging him to sing it on his nationally broadcast weekly radio program. A postscript in the letter to Jolson said that, as a bonus for singing "The Rooster's Crowin'," Marks was sending Jolson a second piece of music he and Caesar had written. Although he did not think it was a par-

1. Chip Deffaa, "Composer's Spotlight on Gerald Marks," *Sheet Music* (January/February, 1990).
2. Ibid.

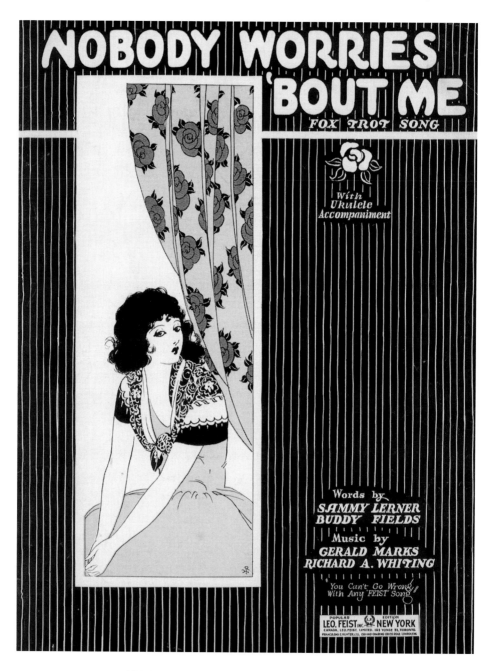

"Nobody Worries 'Bout Me," one of Gerald
Marks's early hits, was written in 1926.

ticularly great song, he felt Jolson could have some fun with it at Hollywood parties.

Soon afterward, Marks received a reply from Jolson—a telegram, telling him to listen to Jolson's next radio show. When Marks turned on his radio, he heard Jolson say he was about to sing a new hit song, written by Marks and Caesar. Instead of announcing "The Rooster's Crowin'," however, Jolson gave the title of the other, "second-rate" song he had been sent. Disappointed and disgusted, Marks turned his radio off and did not even bother to listen to Jolson sing the song. It was not until the next day, when he went to his office, that Marks learned that the song had gone over exceptionally well in its first performance and that he and Caesar had a smash hit, just as Jolson had predicted over the air. Fortunately, Jolson had been a better judge of which of the two songs had the greater potential. He had wisely set aside "The Rooster's Crowin'" and instead had aired "Is It True What They Say about Dixie?" Sheet music sales of this song were enormous and Jolson's subsequent recording of it soon became one of the most famous records ever cut.

Marks wrote a number of other good songs. His irrepressible style and personality are characterized in the unconventional titles he often gave his songs: "They Ought to Give a Letter to Mabel," "Without a Shirt," "Since Lum Come Hum," "Vot Giffs Mit der Dictionary?" "Oh, Suzanna, Dust Off That Old Pianna," "I'm a Fugitive from a Chain Letter Gang," and "I Wish I Had Died at the Altar." Another of his songs in the "unusual title" category, "You're the One, You Beautiful Son-of-a-Gun," drew some criticism when it was first published in 1931. At that time the phrase "son-of-a-gun" was regarded as street language by some people, who apparently equated it with its vicious canine cousin.

In May 1949, the city of Saginaw, whose citizens had been getting their drinking water from pumps strategically located on street corners around town, changed over to a new facility that would pipe in fresh water from a point seventy miles north, in Lake Huron. The new water tasted so much better than the old (which had been tainted with salt and other disagreeable flavors) that the city held a celebration, "The World's Best Water Festival."

The affair was one of the most extensive the community had ever seen. It included a band festival, a rodeo, and a special minor league baseball game featuring the Saginaw Bears. There were dancing exhibitions and contests (jitterbugging for the youngsters, waltzing for their elders), and a parade with thirty-four marching bands and many floats, some with town pumps aboard in honor of the occasion. A ceremonial burial of one

Marks composed "Nothin' to Do But Love" in 1931.

A few people were offended by the phrase "Son-of-a-Gun"
in the title of this 1931 hit by Marks.

"Oh Suzanna, Dust Off That Old Pianna," written in
1935, typifies the exuberance of many of Marks's songs.

Marks's novelty love song, "Saskatchewan," was composed
in 1936. Notice Marks's autograph, left center.

"I Want the Whole World to Love You," a
sentimental ballad, was written by Marks in 1936.

of the old corner pumps was performed in front of the Water Works with the city councilmen serving as pallbearers and Acting City Manager Albert W. Tausend committing the pump to its final resting place. The three-day celebration was capped by a huge Sunday evening fireworks display.

One of the highlights of the festival was the performance of a song Gerald Marks had been commissioned to compose for the occasion, "There Never Was a Place Like Saginaw." The front page of the May 19, 1949, issue of the *Saginaw News* features a picture of two well-known local musicians who performed the song, Marion Newberry and Gertrude Garvin. A copy of the original manuscript for "There Never Was a Place Like Saginaw" is prominently displayed in the background, bearing the inscription, "Words and Music by Gerald Marks."

When writing songs, Marks generally composed the music, and a competent lyricist, such as Sammy Lerner, Seymour Simons, or Irving Caesar, would write the words. One notable exception to this was a song titled "If We Should Never Meet Again." Marks collaborated with lyricist Charles Newman to write the words to this 1934 hit, and the music was composed by none other than Isham Jones.

Like many other songwriters, Marks composed songs outside the realm of popular music that were intended for special use. He put together collections of interdenominational religious music, wrote a number of songs for school children about safety, and composed many patriotic songs. During World War II, the United States Treasury Department used one of his songs, "Dig Down Deep," to urge citizens to purchase war bonds. Along with lyricist Sam Lerner, Marks penned the scores for several musical productions, including *White Horse Inn, Hold It, My Dear Public,* and *Bizzarities.* He also contributed his songwriting talents to *The New Grand Terrace Revue* and *The Ziegfeld Follies.*

Marks also wrote many songs about holidays, ranging from Yom Kippur and Easter to Election Day and Lincoln's Birthday. His holiday songs were written to be enjoyed by young and old alike. Two delightful examples, both written in 1950 with help from fellow songwriter Milton Pascal, are "I Don't Want a Lot for Christmas" and the whimsical Halloween song, "The Wobblin' Goblin (With the Broken Broom)."

Marks put together songs about a great variety of subjects. Like most popular songwriters he composed his share of love songs. But Marks also chose to address many other topics in his music, often in a cheerful, optimistic manner. Marks championed the brotherhood of man with such songs as "There Ain't No Color Line around the Rainbow" and "What Is 'Brotherhood' Week?" Much of his music focuses on the idea of humanity living and working together harmoniously. In pursuit of this noble cause, a number of his songs ridicule the foolishness of ethnic prejudice, without compromising anyone's pride in one's heritage. This was difficult to do, but Marks succeeded in a manner that everyone could enjoy.

Marks was actively involved with ASCAP, having served on its board of directors for many years. One of the activities he pursued on behalf of the organization in his later years was visiting American college campuses and speaking to aspiring student composers about the music publishing business.

In October 1990, at their New York City home, Marks's wife held a surprise party for him, in honor of his ninetieth birthday. Ninety guests attended the celebration. As he recovered from his initial surprise, Marks took a good look at the assembled guests, among whom were some of the most important people in show business. Then, singling out one guest, he walked over to her and introduced her to the group, letting them know how special she was both to him and his wife. The woman was their life-long friend from Saginaw, Ruth Picard, widow of songwriter and judge Frank Picard.

In 1993, Marks presented an autobiographical music revue, "What I Learned in the (Tin Pan) Alley," at the Smithsonian Institution. The following year he entertained President and Mrs. Clinton at a performance at the White House.

Gerald Marks made a significant impact on popular music. Of his many hit songs, the one for which he will undoubtedly be best remembered is "All of Me." A recent release of this song, arranged and played by Mercer Ellington (Duke Ellington's son), was its two thousandth recording, placing it among the most frequently recorded popular songs in history.

Marks passed away early in 1997, at the age of ninety-six. In a final expression of his well-known dynamic sense of humor, he requested that his remains be placed in an urn bearing the epitaph, "All of Me."

Another Marks song of 1936, "Is It True What
They Say about Dixie?" became a hit overnight.

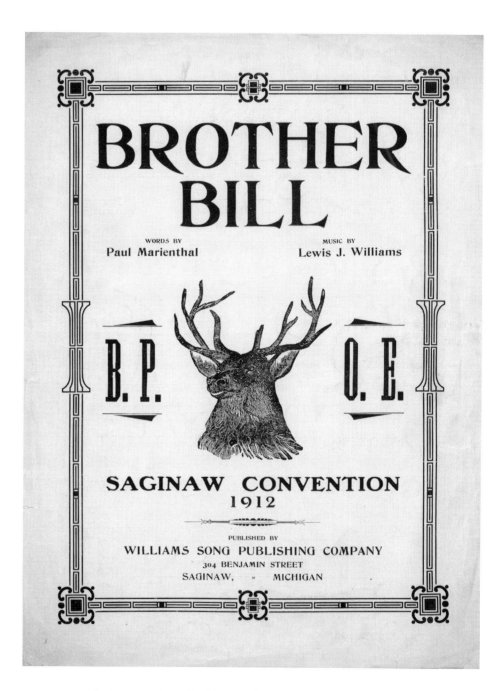

Saginaw residents Paul Marienthal and Lewis Williams wrote
"Brother Bill" for the Elks convention in Saginaw in 1912.

9

⧉ ⧉ ⧉

THEY ALSO SERVED

THERE HAVE BEEN OTHER POPULAR SONGWRITERS from Saginaw whose influence on Tin Pan Alley may not have been as pervasive as that of Charles K. Harris, Isham Jones, or Gerald Marks, but who, nonetheless, have made significant contributions to American popular music. Among these individuals were Lewis J. Williams, Paul Marienthal, Nels Bitterman, Blanche Northrup, Phebe Callaghan, Harold Berg, Josef Cherney, Walter Kremer, Elmer Patton, Ernest Miller, Howard "Howdy" Quicksell, John Chalmers "Chummy" MacGregor, Clara Vervoort, Dorothy Knodel, Susaine Wheeler, Marguerite Bosley, Mary F. Way, John Nauer, Jack Hedrick, Jack Robinson, and Eugene "Gene" Fernett.

In the early 1900s, Lewis J. Williams, then a sales manager at Saginaw's B. G. Appleby Company (which specialized in home building and real estate sales), wrote a few popular songs which he published in Saginaw. Among these were "Dear Little Pal," "Why Don't Santa Claus Come Here?" "Little Dutch Lunch," and a romantic Irish Ballad, "Nora Machree." Inside the front cover of "Nora Machree" is a B. G. Appleby Company ad stating, "We have For Sale 150 ready built houses ranging in price from $450 to $10,000."

In 1912, Williams collaborated with Saginaw travel agent Paul Marienthal to write a march song titled "Brother Bill," in honor of the Elks convention held in Saginaw that year. Displaying a picture of an elk on its front cover, "Brother Bill" was well written and featured some highly spirited words and music.

Williams later moved to Toledo, Ohio, where he became known as "The Buckeye Poet." In addition to his literary ventures, he was closely

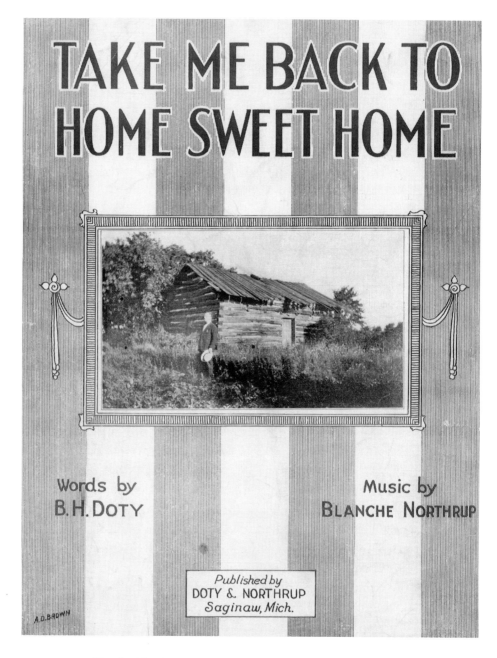

Blanche Northrup, a church organist, wrote "Take Me Back
to Home Sweet Home" in 1921. (Used by permission.)

involved in working with underprivileged boys, and he served as Super-intendent of the Toledo Newsboys Association. During this time, the boys of that organization, under Williams's direction, published a newspaper to which the *New York World* awarded a prize for being the best newspaper of its kind in the world.

Nelson "Nels" Bitterman's first public appearances as a musician were with his brother Archie's dance band and with Arthur Amsden's 33rd Regimental Band. In 1923, Nels moved from Saginaw to Detroit, where he worked as a drummer, playing in various dance bands for the next twenty years. During the early 1920s he wrote "I'm a Specialist," which became popular and was recorded by Frank Krumit on the Victor label. In 1940, Bitterman was hired as a draftsman by a Detroit engineering firm. He continued working in this capacity until his retirement in 1970.

Blanche Northrup, who was the organist and choir director at Saginaw's old Warren Avenue Methodist Church for many years, earned a reputation as a composer of hymns. In 1921, she also succeeded in writing something a little more on the secular side: "Take Me Back to Home Sweet Home." Northrup was also well known as a teacher of organ and piano and remained active in this role until the age of ninety-three, when she was still working with three students. She lived to the remarkable age of one-hundred-five.

In 1922, Phebe Grant Callaghan, a Saginaw resident who billed herself "Authoress, Composer of Song, Poems, and Writer of Orations," composed and published a song called simply "Saginaw." The piece was advertised as a fox-trot (a common dance of the Tin Pan Alley era) but was more like a school song or patriotic number. The piece was not very danceable but the lyrics did a remarkably good job of extolling the virtues of the composer's hometown. A photo on the song's front cover features Saginaw's Hoyt Library and the old Castle Post Office (now the Saginaw County Historical Museum).

Harold C. Berg was born in Saginaw in 1900. He attended the Saginaw schools until his family moved to Detroit, where he completed high school. Working as a lyricist, he wrote the words to a number of popular songs in the 1920s and early 1930s. His best-known effort was "Freshie," written in 1925, with composer Jesse Greer furnishing the music. Berg served as a staff lyricist for Warner Brothers Studios in Hollywood during the 1930s and later worked as a public relations consultant in Detroit.

"The Bells of Avalon," written in 1927 by Josef Cherniavsky,
enjoyed some popularity for many years.

Josef Cherney was born in Russia in 1895, moved to the United States shortly after the Russian Revolution, and came to Saginaw about 1951. Although his musical orientation was strongly classical (he had studied with the great Russian masters Alexander Glazounov and Nikolai Rimsky-Korsakov) Cherney composed a nice piece of popular music in 1927, "The Bells of Avalon." Eminent lyricist Mitchell Parish liked the song well enough to contribute his talents as lyricist. "The Bells of Avalon" never became a big hit, but it never completely faded from the popular music scene either, and it is still heard once in a while.

Cherney scored some music for the motion picture industry, and contributed at least one song, "Love Sings a Song in My Heart," to the great movie musical by Jerome Kern and Oscar Hammerstein II, *Show Boat*. In addition to writing a number of other popular songs, he also worked on the score for an operetta, *Pink Lemonade,* which contained pieces with such contrasting titles as "Petite Waltz" and "Bachanale in a Chicken Coop."

Cherney was actually a pen name he sometimes used early in his composing career. Saginaw audiences knew him later as Josef Cherniavsky (his real name), the conductor of the Saginaw Symphony Orchestra for a number of years.

Walter F. Kremer, like Cherniavsky, also had a formal musical background. He studied at the Chicago Institute of Music, and played cello and viola with the Saginaw Germania Symphony Orchestra. A versatile musician, Kremer also played trumpet with dance bands in the Saginaw area and served as pianist and director of the Jeffers-Strand Vaudeville House Orchestra during World War I. In 1929, he wrote "Those Were the Days" and published it himself in Saginaw. Most of Kremer's later career was spent as a music teacher.

Elmer G. Patton, who later headed the E. G. Patton Food Brokerage in Saginaw, worked as a lyricist during the 1920s and early 1930s. Several of his songs were popularized by singer Rudy Vallee. Patton enjoyed a diversified career. Before writing words to popular music, he had worked in a lumber camp, for a Great Lakes shipping firm, and as a Hollywood extra, playing bit parts in early motion pictures.

Ernest Miller never had any music instruction, and for some time he played completely by ear. Eventually, however, he acquired sufficient familiarity with written music to write successful arrangements for some of the dance bands that played in and around Saginaw. Miller composed "How

Howard "Howdy" Quicksell wrote the words
to "You Are Just a Vision" in 1925.

Could I Be Blue?" in 1930 and "Where the Roses Are So Beautiful (There's a Home for You and Me)" in 1932.

Before going into the insurance business in Saginaw, Howard "Howdy" Quicksell was known to traditional jazz enthusiasts as a highly capable tenor banjo player who worked with many of the greatest jazz musicians of the 1920s and early 1930s. Among these greats were Bix Beiderbecke, Frankie Trumbauer, Joe Venuti, Eddie Lang, Wingy Manone, Jimmy and Tommy Dorsey, and Jean Goldkette.

While playing with Goldkette's band Quicksell first met Ange Lorenzo, who was playing piano with the group. Later, in Saginaw, Quicksell and Lorenzo worked together again—this time writing songs rather than playing them. Quicksell also wrote some songs by himself, his best-known efforts being "Since My Best Girl Turned Me Down" and "Sorry," both recorded by Beiderbecke and his band on Okeh records, and "The Way I Feel Today," recorded on the Victor label by McKinney's Cotton Pickers. Another song, "You Are Just a Vision," was the result of a collaborative effort by several members of Goldkette's band, including Quicksell and Goldkette himself.

John Chalmers "Chummy" MacGregor was born in Saginaw in 1903. After attending the Saginaw schools, he went to the University of Michigan, where he majored in music. He played in various dance bands in Detroit, Chicago, and New York before moving to Paris in 1927, where he scored music for revues at the Café des Ambassadeurs. He moved back to America in 1932, where he played with the Smith Ballew Band for three years. While working with this organization he befriended a young trombonist named Glenn Miller. Later, when Miller formed his own group, he invited MacGregor to come with him. MacGregor achieved his greatest fame with this legendary big band, serving as pianist and arranger from 1936 to 1942.

During the 1930s and 1940s, MacGregor wrote the music for a number of songs, the best known being "It Must Be Jelly ('Cause Jam Don't Shake Like That)" and the theme song used by Miller's Air Force Band, "I Sustain the Wings." He also scored music for several films that featured the Miller Band, including *Sun Valley Serenade, Orchestra Wives,* and *The Glenn Miller Story.*

In 1940, suburban Saginaw homemaker Clara Vervoort wrote both words and music to " 'Cause I'm Idiotic Over You." Prominently displayed on the front cover of this song is a photograph of Paul Nielsen, whose band introduced the piece at Saginaw's Moonlight Gardens Night Club.

Vervoort employed a simple, yet pleasant melody in creating this song, and her lyrics were cleverly conceived.

In 1942, three homemakers who lived in Bridgeport, a suburb of Saginaw, got together to write a patriotic song, "Our V for Victory." Collaborating to write this highly spirited piece honoring American servicemen and women were Dorothy L. Knodel, Susaine P. Wheeler, and Marguerite W. Bosley.

Mary F. Way worked for Baker Perkins of Saginaw for forty-seven years as an executive secretary. In 1937, she wrote the words and music to "It Was Nice to Have Known You," and, ten years later, "It's a Man's World." For someone who wrote only two pieces of popular music, Mary Way's songs exhibit a remarkably mature (and pleasing) style. It is unfortunate that she did not write more. She now resides in suburban Saginaw.

In June 1942, Mrs. Clarence J. Nauer of Saginaw received a piece of music in the mail from her son, Private John B. Nauer, then serving with the U.S. Army in Australia and New Guinea. The song, written by Nauer and published earlier that year in Australia, was a patriotic number titled "The Aussies and the Yanks Are Here." The cover features a photograph of Nauer, between Australian and American flags. The song was on Australia's Hit Parade for two years, holding the number one spot for sixteen consecutive weeks.

During the late 1930s, Johnny Nauer had gone to New York and had tried to break into the fiercely competitive popular songwriting market. Unfortunately, his style had not yet matured, and the publishing houses there were not interested in the material he had to offer, although he was encouraged to keep trying by several publishers who recognized his potential. Somewhat discouraged, Nauer returned home to Saginaw and, after some time, decided to join the Army. He still worked on songwriting, however, using a ukulele (which was easy to carry around) to try out new musical ideas. In Australia, where Nauer and his unit were stationed, Lieutenant Joe Weisenberger, the director of a U.S. Army musical group, heard Nauer sing "The Aussies and the Yanks Are Here." Weisenberger had the song arranged for his group, they performed it, and Johnny Nauer had a hit on his hands.

Before long, he had written the words and music to three more songs, all of which became hits in Australia: "Say a Prayer," "I Found a Princess

Clara Vervoort wrote "'Cause I'm Idiotic
Over You" in 1940. (Used by permission.)

In 1942, Johnny Nauer wrote about the camaraderie between the
Australian and American servicemen during World War II, in
"The Aussies and the Yanks Are Here." This copy bears
a personal note from Nauer to his parents.

in Queensland," and "Fuzzy Wuzzy Angels." Not only had Nauer's song-writing style matured, but he was also able to give the public what they wanted when they wanted it. It was ironic that he had to go halfway around the world to find success as a songwriter, a fact not overlooked by Lowell Thomas, the well-known newscaster and commentator of World War II. Thomas devoted an entire radio program one evening to Nauer's unusual success story. After the war, Nauer returned to Saginaw and pursued a successful career in journalism, first with the *Saginaw News,* and later with the *Midland Daily News,* where he rose to the position of managing editor.

Another song that came out of World War II was "Adolf," written and published by John "Jack" P. Hedrick of Saginaw, in 1942. Hedrick, who was president and general manager of Seeman and Peters (a Saginaw printing and advertising firm) wrote the words and music to this humorous song which related, in some detail, how the United States and its Allies were planning to send German dictator Adolf Hitler to a permanent residence well known for its eternally warm climate.

Also in 1942, Sally Logan Volz, a school music teacher and choir director who had earlier been a Saginaw resident, wrote both the words and music to another patriotic song, "Keep in Step." Proceeds from sales of copies of this song were used to purchase United States war savings bonds.

Other popular songs to come from the pens of Saginaw songwriters at about this time were Irene Turnbull Mikolaizyk's "There's a Ring Around My Finger (and a Glow Around My Heart), written in 1945, and "Teasing Me" (1946) by Saginaw residents Harold Roeser and Archie Zander.

In 1949, Jack Robinson, a machine operator at Eaton Manufacturing Company in Saginaw, wrote "Gee, I Wish I Was Rich." The lyrics of this song focus on the wistful daydreams of a working man who feels his life is circumscribed by the demands of his work schedule. Like Mary Way's songs, Robinson's song was featured in one of the Saginaw Quota Club's annual *Show Boat* variety productions. In addition to several other songs, Robinson also wrote some poetry and fiction.

Eugene "Gene" Fernett was probably best known for his work with big bands during the latter part of the Tin Pan Alley era and for a few years afterward. In addition to being a band leader, trombonist, and arranger, he composed a number of pieces for big bands. He also was a writer of feature articles about a variety of topics, and the author of a book about the big bands, bearing the same title as one of his compositions, *A Thousand Golden Horns.*

10

⊞　⊞　⊞

CUTTING A SUIT AND STILL WRITING SONGS

THE TERM "SEGUE," as applied in music, indicates that the performer is to continue, without pause, even though the mood or style of the selection being performed may change significantly. There is probably no songwriter who comes closer to personifying the word segue in moving successfully from the waning Tin Pan Alley era into other styles of music than Ben Weisman.

Weisman was born in Providence, Rhode Island. As a boy, he moved with his family to what was known at that time as the Sunrise Colony, on the old Prairie Farm, near the village of Alicia, about eight miles south of Saginaw. There he took lessons from Saginaw piano teacher Grace Perry Watson, who recognized young Weisman's exceptional talent, and who provided him with guidance and encouragement to pursue a career in music.

As a young man, Weisman studied piano and composition at Juilliard, hoping to become a concert pianist or composer. He discovered, however, that there were few opportunities to make a living in this manner. He began exploring other musical directions, and eventually studied jazz piano with Benny Goodman's great pianist, Teddy Wilson, and worked as an accompanist for Eddie Fisher, Vic Damone, the Ames Brothers, and others. He was a successful performing artist, but as Weisman himself said, "I was doing well, but my heart was in writing." Once he decided to write songs, he had little desire to concentrate on performing them.

Weisman's first published song was "Makes a Difference to My Heart," in 1947. His first hit, "Have a Little Sympathy" (1949), was recorded by Dean Martin and the Gordon Jenkins Orchestra, and was also sung by Dennis Day on Jack Benny's radio show. At about this time Weisman began collaborating with lyricist Fred Wise. Mitch Miller, then an executive with Columbia Records, began using Weisman's and Wise's songs with singers Doris Day, Frankie Laine, Johnny Ray, and Guy Mitchell.

In 1954, Weisman and Wise were asked to adapt a song written by country composer Jenny Lou Carson for use in the popular CBS television anthology show *Studio One*. The producers of the show liked Carson's song, but they felt it needed a little more sophistication. The song, originally titled "Let Me Go, Devil," was smoothed out in the appropriate places by Weisman and Wise and given a new title, "Let Me Go, Lover." It became an overnight hit.

By the end of 1955 Weisman had written nearly two hundred songs. At about that time the Tin Pan Alley years were coming to a close. Unlike most cultural changes, this process was rapid, as the decision makers at music publishing houses and recording companies quickly realized there was far greater profit in catering to the tastes of suddenly affluent teenagers than to those of more conservatively spending adults. American popular music soon turned in a new direction. Weisman continued to write some popular music along traditional lines, but he found it much easier to earn a living by giving his publishers (and through them, the paying public) what they wanted. His talent and training enabled him to branch out in many musical directions, including jazz, country, gospel, rhythm and blues, big band, and rock. It was with the latter that he attained his greatest recognition, particularly as the composer of fifty-seven songs sung by Elvis Presley which sold more than a million records each. Among these hits were "Got a Lot of Livin' to Do," "Don't Ask Me Why," "Fame and Fortune," and "As Long as I Have You." Weisman also holds the distinction of having written songs for every one of Presley's movies.

The list of performers who have presented Weisman's music to the public is a virtual "Who's Who" in popular music. This list includes the singers and bands named above, as well as singers Barbra Streisand, Dionne Warwick, Gladys Knight, Cher, Reba McEntire, Sarah Vaughn, Peggy Lee, Teresa Brewer, Patti Page, June Valli, Georgia Gibbs, Dinah Shore, Connie Francis, Sammy Davis Jr., Perry Como, Nat "King" Cole, Billy Eckstein, Vaughn Monroe, Jimmy Dean, Johnny Mathis, the Pointer Sisters, the Carpenters, the Four Aces, the Beatles, the Statler Brothers, the Sons of the Pioneers, and the Mills Brothers. Also the bands or orchestras of Woody Herman, Sammy Kaye, Ray Anthony, Ray Coniff, Xavier Cugat, Buddy Morrow, Ray Block, Jackie Gleason, Ralph Flanagan, and Lionel Hampton have performed and recorded Weisman's songs.

Weisman has written music featured in no fewer than thirty motion pictures, including the Academy Award–winning "The Young Americans," which earned an Oscar as the best feature-length documentary film of 1965. Perhaps the most spectacular composing he has ever done synthesized elements of rock and symphonic music in his twenty-minute long "Concerto for Elvis," written in 1980. The three-movement work, scored for orchestra and a rock combo of guitar, bass, and drums, is based on three songs of Weisman's that Presley had recorded: "As Long As I Have You," "Crawfish," and "I Slipped, I Stumbled, I Fell." This work was later adapted for ballet by choreographer Anne Marie de Angelo.

In an interview with Daniel T. Walker, of the National Academy of Songwriters, Weisman made some interesting comments regarding any conflict he might feel writing rock songs, given his formal musical background. "If you want to be in the top ten," he said, "you can't let your personal tastes control you . . . I studied [Presley's] style closely . . . and I wrote and arranged for him to suit his style. It was like cutting a suit." With regard to his continued success after the Tin Pan Alley era, Weisman said, "I'm a craftsman and I know how to cross over. That's why I'm still going. . . . It's important for songwriters to realize the importance of being able to write in different styles."[1] This brings to mind a phrase used at the dawn of the Tin Pan Alley era, in a critique of a song written in 1894: "well designed to meet public favor."

A vigorous, friendly individual, Weisman is still active in the music business. He and his wife live in Marina Del Ray, California. He still values his ties to the Saginaw area. In 1991 he made a trip to Saginaw to visit the old Prairie Farm, where he had lived and studied music with Grace Perry Watson, "just to relive some old memories."

1. Author interview with Ben Weisman, Saginaw, 1991.

11

⊠　⊠　⊠

FINALE

THERE HAVE BEEN MANY INDIVIDUALS FROM SAGINAW who have made significant contributions in other fields of music. Jazz saxophone great Edward "Sonny" Stitt; bass player Larry Angell of the Cleveland Symphony Orchestra; composer Roland Trogan; rock singer and songwriter Stevie Wonder; jazz arranger Kenny Anderson; and John Krell, who played flute with the Philadelphia Orchestra, are only a few of them. It was through the songs of Tin Pan Alley, however, that Saginaw musicians touched the lives of the greatest number of people and left their most enduring legacy.

Not only have Saginaw's Tin Pan Alley songwriters given us their music, they have also provided us with an opportunity to examine the manner in which popular music in America has reflected the nature of the time in which it was written, and how it has changed, accordingly.

Starting in the late Victorian period, songwriters poured forth a veritable deluge of tear-jerking, heart-rending ballads. Then, moving into a more relaxed era, popular music began to lose its more inhibitive nature and people began to have fun with it. This was an experimental time for popular music: the jazz age was beginning and a growing nationalism crept into the music of the time. Next came the 1920s, when a pleasant blend of highly syncopated dance tunes and wonderful ballads appeared. This mixed fare seemed to satisfy the listening and dancing public well into the 1930s, while gradually increasing in musical sophistication. Then, with the Swing era and the big band movement at their height, along came World War II. With the war came a number of patriotic songs, mixed with sentimental ballads. Finally, with the happy turbulence that immediately followed World War II, Tin Pan Alley enjoyed its last hurrah. By the late 1950s, it was no longer a significant factor in American entertainment.

Saginaw's role in the history of Tin Pan Alley was remarkable. Not many cities of its size can boast of having influenced the formative years in the musical lives of so many successful songwriters—composers and lyricists of the caliber of Arthur McWatters, Joseph Hughes, Fred Cummins, Harry Richardson, Dan Russo, Carl Rupp, Ole Olsen, Harold Berg, Chummy MacGregor, and Johnny Nauer—not to mention Gerald Marks and Ben Weisman, who have made so many outstanding contributions to American popular music. Few if any other communities of comparable size can lay claim to two Tin Pan Alley men whose stature rivals that of Charles K. Harris and Isham Jones. Although neither Harris nor Jones was born in Saginaw, nor did either of them die there, they both grew to adulthood and developed their musical tastes and abilities there. Each represented the best that popular music had to offer during their respective times in history.

Harris turned out a great number of popular songs, ranging in quality from good to fair (by present-day standards). Harris's greatest strengths lay in his ability to judge just what the public wanted to hear, and in having the musical aptitude to respond appropriately. Combining these abilities with his exceptionally keen business sense, he was able to turn every enterprise he undertook into financial profit.

Once Harris had identified a song topic that sold successfully, he would continue to address that topic in subsequent songs until there was little remaining unsaid on the subject. He would sometimes even employ this "composition by formula" philosophy in selecting titles for his songs. Notice, for example, the similarities in the titles of " 'Mid the Green Fields of Virginia," "In the Hills of Old Carolina," and " 'Mid the Blue Grass of Kentucky." In 1915, he even duplicated the title of a song he had written in 1891, "School Bells," despite using different words and music for these two songs.

Also, Harris never passed up an opportunity to advertise his musical wares. When he opened his own publishing house almost every piece of sheet music he published had a page or two devoted to lists of his previous compositions, with the purchase price of each piece listed alongside the title. At times he even went so far as to include titles of songs he had previously written in the lyrics of new songs he composed.[1]

---

1. In the chorus of "The Organ-Grinder's Serenade," which Harris wrote in 1897, he used both the music and the lyrics from the title lines of "After the Ball" (published in 1892) and "Creep, Baby, Creep" (1890). Harris's "Songs of Yesterday" (1916) was an unabashed, undisguised effort to adver-

We can, however, forgive Harris for seemingly putting musical commercialism before creativity when we remember that he was the first of his kind, creating and exploring a new musical genre. We might refer to him as the musical Columbus who discovered Tin Pan Alley. If Harris had not coupled attention to sales with his compositional efforts, the popular music publishing business, or Tin Pan Alley, might never have taken the direction it did, and it might never have played such an important role in the history of American entertainment. Other significant accomplishments by Harris include his work in organizing ASCAP and his contributions to copyright law, resulting in many benefits to composers, as well as to authors and publishers.

Although he did not write as many songs as Harris did, and did not possess Harris's business acumen, Isham Jones wrote a great number of popular songs. He seemed to have had the Midas touch in the music he composed: almost everything he wrote was pure gold, musically speaking. He never found it necessary to resort to any gimmickry or short cuts. Jones's compositions were of a quality that has seldom been equaled in the history of popular music. In short, he refined the art of popular songwriting. Additionally, Jones's accomplishments as a performer, bandleader, and arranger cannot be overlooked. Just as Harris had pioneered the early popular music field, Jones was unsurpassed in his innovations as an arranger and in his influence in determining the nature and direction of the modern American dance band.

It is easy to understand why Harris and Jones are regarded as two of the most important figures in the history of Tin Pan Alley. They were, however, men of different eras. Their music spoke to the tastes of people whose lives were being shaped by different social conditions and historical processes.

Determining how one community could produce such a wealth of songwriting talent is not a simple matter. There were two important influences, however, that played major roles in the occurrence of this phenomenon.

tise his music, apparently hoping to strike a responsive chord in the hearts of some of the older members of the public, who would remember his songs from an earlier era. This unusual song features excerpts from the following Harris compositions: "Would You Care?" (1905), "I'm Wearing My Heart Away for You" (1902), "'Mid the Green Fields of Virginia" (1898), "In the Vale of Shenandoah" (1904), "Fallen by the Wayside" (1892), "Break the News to Mother" (1897), "I Love Her Just the Same" (1896), "Always in the Way" (1903), "There'll Come a Time" (1895), "Somewhere" (1906), and "After the Ball." On the front cover of "Songs of Yesterday" is a portrait of Harris, surrounded by copies of the covers of eight of these songs. Taking aim at the new, syncopated songs that were taking the place of his "heart story ballad hits," Harris wrote, in the first verse of "Songs of Yesterday," "All you hear today is ragtime and the same old tango tunes. How I long to hear the songs of yesterday."

One of these influences, around the turn of the century, arose from a rapidly growing cultural awareness in and around Saginaw, which resulted in the development of a powerful musical presence in the community. This attracted many accomplished musicians to the area, among whom were numerous outstanding teachers of music, such as Albert W. Platte, John Grinnell Cummins, Louis C. Toepel, Napoleon S. Lagatree, Samuel Richard Gaines, John Prindle Scott, William A. Boos, and Arthur D. Amsden.[2] These teachers, in turn, conveyed their musical knowledge and enthusiasm to a generation of young Saginaw musicians, many of whom became successful songwriters.

The other major influence, going back to the latter part of Saginaw's lumbering era, was imparted by the many traveling musicians who passed through town and left their mark on Saginaw's impressionable youngsters—young people who were thrilled and inspired by the musicians' performances, and who would finally grow up to constitute a remarkable generation of songwriters. As a 1948 article in the *Saginaw News* stated, "These honky-tonks of the lumbering days were the starting place for many persons who reached the pinnacles of success in the show world."

As it is with many areas today, the Saginaw Valley's natural resources—its vast pine forests—are now depleted. There is, however, something significant from Saginaw's colorful past that will remain with us for a long time: the abundant legacy of songs from the pens of Saginaw's many wonderful lyricists and composers of popular music. To paraphrase the first line from an Irving Berlin song, Tin Pan Alley has ended, but the melodies linger on.

---

2. In 1894 there were 52 music teachers listed in Saginaw's classified business directory; in 1909, there were 77. This is in dramatic contrast with the 1997 classified telephone directory's listing of three Saginaw locations offering music lessons, especially considering the current larger population base.

APPENDIX ONE

Biographical Data about Saginaw Songwriters

The Saginaw residences listed below for each songwriter have been documented in the East Saginaw and Saginaw city directories published between 1868 and 1958. If a songwriter's name appears in the text, but not in this table, it is because no additional biographical data could be found.

Amsden, Arthur D. (1865–1926)
325 Owen; 1022 Hoyt

Berg, Harold C. (1900–1973)

Bitterman, Nels (1903–)
715 Lapeer

Boardman, George
616 S. Washington

Boos, William A. (1865–1959)
808 Lapeer; 522 S. Warren

Bosley, Marguerite W.
Bridgeport

Brockman, James (1886–1967)
618 S. Washington(?)

Callaghan, Phebe G.
1121 Holland

Cherniavsky, Josef (1895–1959)
117 S. Mason

Cintura, Joseph (1838–1904)

Corbit, Clarence
704 N. Michigan

Cummings, John G. (1858–1935)
210 Sheridan; 235 N. Jefferson

Cummins, Fred C. (c. 1885–)
2216 Ames (now Avon)

Erd, Frank H. (1863–1896)
231 S. Third; 223 S. Fourth;
524 Genesee

Fernett, Eugene "Gene"
(1924–1987)
1508 Court

Fogg, Elmer E. (1861–)
1204 Burt; 306 S. Washington

Gaines, Samuel R. (1869–1945)
724 S. Park; 310 S. Washington

Grant, George (1852–1942)
1002 S. Jefferson

Harper, Mamie A.
220 King

Harris, Charles K. (1867–1930)
200 block, N. Warren; Bancroft
House hotel

Hedrick, Jack (1906–)
214 N. Franklin; 24 Hanchett
(now Benton)

Hughes, Joseph H. (c. 1885–)
2643 N. Michigan

Hurst, Lewis E. (1882–1976)
104 N. Hamilton

Jaeger, Felix
910 Thompson

Jones, Isham (1894–1956)
202 Wells; 1403 Bliss

Knodel, Dorothy L. (n.d.–1974)
Bridgeport

Kremer, Walter F. (1893–1962)
1805 Janes; 1107 Walnut;
2037 Walnut

Lagatree, Napoleon (c. 1860–)
433 Hanchett

Lorenzo, Ange (1894–1971)
2621 State; 1710 State

**MacGregor, John Chalmers
"Chummy"** (1903–1973)
107 N. Oakley; 1636 Genesee;
1115 S. Jefferson

Marienthal, Paul
616 Johnson; 108 S. Washington

Marks, Gerald (1900–1997)
620 S. Fifth

McWatters, Arthur (c. 1875–)
1500 S. Hamilton

Mikolaizyk, Irene Turnbull M.
407 S. Warren; 1330 High;
827 S. Jefferson

Miller, Ernest (1905–)
802 N. Mason

Nauer, John B. (1915–1986)
508 Hill; Wadsworth Road

Norris, Alfred W. (1875–1957)
1144 Genesee; 1150 Genesee

Norris, Charles M. (1849–1900)
1144 Genesee

Norris, Harold J. (c. 1880–)
1144 Genesee

Norris, James H.
Warren, near Fitzhugh

Northrup, Blanche (1891–1996)
2064 Mackinaw

Olsen, Ole (1894–1956)
613 Brockway (now 1513)

Patton, Elmer G. (1898–1996)
1902 Brenner; 2411 Adams Blvd.

Picard, Frank (1889–1963)
619 Atwater; 1103 E. Genesee;
1600 Cedar

Platte, Albert W. (1860–1916)
537 Millard

Pulfrey, Herbert G.
914 Genesee; 415 N. Washington

Quicksell, Howdy (1900–1953)
1007 Congress; 2835 State

Richardson, Harry (c. 1885–1930)
723 Howard

Robinson, Jack (1916–)
3239 Glasby

Roeser, Harold (1892–1969)
921 Cass

Roney, Henry B.
813 S. Washington

Roney, Thomas C. (c. 1850–)
near 1401 S. Water; 813 S.
Washington

Ruifrok, Henri W. J. (1862–1933)
411 N. Franklin

Rupp, Carl (1893–)
917 Federal

Russo, Danny (1886–1956)
228 N. 6th

Schaefer, Charles B. (1903–)
122 S. 6th

Scott, John P. (1877–1932)
326 S. Jefferson

Toepel, Louis C.
516 S. Porter

Turner, Harry
117 N. Warren; 215 N. Weadock

Tyler, Saleu L.
125 S. Washington

Van Loon, J. (c. 1850–)
516 Franklin

Vervoort, Clara (1902–1985)
9520 East Road

Way, Mary F. (1917–)
603 N. Michigan; 1556 Sullivan

Weisman, Ben
Prairie Farm, Alicia

Wheat, Isaac C. V.
Washington at Carroll; Bancroft House

Wheeler, Susaine P.
Bridgeport

Williams, Lewis J. (1871?–)
1124 Germania; 304 Benjamin

Wondree, Louis H.
1825 Genesee; 511 Marquette

Zander, Archie
2305 S. Washington

Explanatory Notes for Appendices 2 and 3

The date of earliest publication of each song is provided where known. Songs marked with an asterisk (*) bear titles that are similar or identical to those of better-known songs by other songwriters. The song titles listed in appendices 2 and 3 do not constitute a list of the complete works of any of the composers or lyricists listed. These are simply the titles of the popular songs written by these songwriters that the author was able to document. In most cases each songwriter probably produced many more songs than are listed here.

Two exceptions are Gerald Marks and Ben Weisman; their popular songs are listed in Appendix 3. They gave ASCAP their written permission to send the author a comprehensive list of most of their published music.

APPENDIX TWO

Partial List of Secular Music by Early Saginaw Composers Who Helped Pave the Way for Tin Pan Alley

Amsden, Arthur D.

The Death of Custer (1915)
General Boucher March (1916)
Pep (1917)
Follow the Band (1918)
General Boardman March (1919)
(The Tourist) in Florida (1924)
Peppers (1924)
Colonel Bates March
Echo Polka
More Pep
Saginaw, My Saginaw
Two Pieces for Two Euphoniums

Boos, William A.

Gay Masqueraders (1900)
The United States Secret Service
    March (1942)
The 3275

Cabot, H. C.

Capitol Guards Polka-Marzuka
    (1876)

Corbit, Clarence

The Assembly March (1926)

Cummings, John Grinnell

Humming Birds (1910)
Ecstasy (1923)
In the Gloaming* (1923)

The Flag of Freedom
Moon Magic

Erd, Frank H.

Erd's Music House Schottische
    (1890)

Fogg, Elmer E.

Lily of the Valley Waltz
Zig Zag Gallop

Gaines, Samuel Richard

Good-night, Marie (1892)
Adoration (1917)
The Likes of Her
The Mother-Heart
O Victorious People
Of All the Year, 'Tis Summer
Out Where the West Begins
The Owl Courtship
Sweetheart
The Village Blacksmith
Youth!

Harper, Mamie A.
    See Hurst, Lewis E.

**Hurst, Lewis E., with
    Mamie A. Harper**

By the Beautiful Old Saginaw
    (1909)

153

Jenness, Rhea

Nu Gamma Nu March and Two-
Step (1900)

Lagatree, Napoleon S.

In Idle Moments (1897)
La Tipica Polka
Loin Du Bal*
Mao Waltz

Norris, Alfred W.

Krinolin Two-Step (1894)
Twentieth-Century Woman
(1896)
Fair Detective (1897)
Saginaw Carnival March (1898)
Saginaw Street Fair March
(1898?)

**Norris, Alfred W., with Harold J.
Norris**

A Little Brunette Dressed in Pink
(1901)

Norris, Charles Merrill Norris

Lonely Hours (1870)
Lost Oleane (1871)
Dreamland Wanderings (1872)
Don Quixote March (1875)
The Red Ribbon March (1877)
The No Name Waltz (1885)
East Saginaw Grand March
(1888?)
Aristocracy Waltzes (1895)

Norris, Harold J.
See also Norris, Alfred W.

The Home Comers (March and
Two-Step) (1907)

Platte, Albert W.

Ah, 'Tis a Dream (1898)

Queen of the Saginaw Valley
(1907)

Pulfrey, Herbert G.

Jolly Friends March and Two-Step
(1897)
Francesca Waltzes (1902)
Lizzette Waltzes (1903)
Zurita (A Mexican Dance) (1903)
Peddler's Parade (1905)
Caroline (A March Song and
Two-Step) (1906)
Auto Girl March and Two-Step
(1906)
Red Hots: March and Two-Step
(1907)
The Cable March and Two-Step
(1909)
Ann Harbour March
Mexican Dance
Yankee Kids

Reed, Benjamin F. *See Rieder,
Grace*

**Rieder, Grace, with Benjamin F.
Reed**

Hurrah Again for Teddy (1912)

Roney, Henry B.

Rifle Waltzes (1876)

Roney, Thomas C.

Psi Upsilon Waltz (1875)

Ruifrok, Henri W. J.

A Dear Little "Somebody" (1895)
Good Night
I Love Him
I Love You
Love
Snow Flakes
Thou Art So Like a Flower
Thy Remembrance

Schaefer, Charles B.

The Devil's Delight (1894)

Scott, John Prindle

The Wind's in the South (1916)
At the Donnybrook Fair (1917)
The Top o' the Mornin' (1917?)
Dennis and Norah (1917?)
Ride On! Ride On! (1918)
To an Old Love (1919)
The Old Road (1920)
Spray o' Heather (1921)
The Maid of Japan (1921)
The False Prophet (The Lying
    Little Daisy) (1922)
Good Luck, Mister Fisherman
    (1922)
Love Is a Riddle (1928)
The Dearest Place
Getting Started
Holiday
In Canterbury Square
John o' Dreams
The Likes o' Him
Old Bill Bluff
One Gave Me a Rose

Riverside Park Reverie
Romeo in Georgia
The Secret
Trelawney
Young Alan the Piper

Toepel, Louis C.

Waldo March (1893)
Your Mother's Heart (1894)

Turner, Harry

Light Infantry March and Two-
    Step (1894)

Tyler, Saleu L.

Only a Brook (1872)

Van Loon, J.

Bootblack's Whistle Waltz (1875)

Wondree, Louis Harold

The Gallant Brigade (Military
    March and Two-Step (1914)
The Trials of Love (1914)
My Country Needs Me,
    Sweetheart, I Must Go (1914)

APPENDIX THREE

Partial List of Tin Pan Alley Music by Saginaw Songwriters

Berg, Harold C.

Mary-Ellen (Since I Fell in Love with You) (1922)

Holding Hands (1923)

Slumbering (1923)

Dreamy Chinee (1923?)

It Might Have Been Me (1924)

Mine (Through All the Years to Come) (1924)

Old Fashioned Rose (1924)

Freshie (1925)

If It Wasn't for You, I Wouldn't be Crying Now (1934)

Dream Boat

Hi Jinx

I'll Remember

It Never Will Happen Again

Kickin' Up the Dust

Mon Paris à Moi

My Little Home

Parting Kiss

Stairway to Happiness

Susan

Sweetheart Lane

This Is Our Busy Day

This Is the Last Time

We'll Always Have Tonight to Remember

When We Are Millionaires

You Left Me Nothing But Mem'ries

Bitterman, Nelson "Nels"

I'm a Specialist

Bosley, Marguerite W.
See Wheeler, Susaine P.

Brockman, James

Write, Wire or Telephone (1907)

When the Roses Kissed the Autumn Leaves Good Bye (1907)

My Fluff-a de Ruff (1908)

Some One Else (1908)

If I Could Gain the World by Wishing (I Would Only Wish for You) (1908)

Abie, Take an Example from Your Father (1908?)

Waylo (1908?)

Wop, Wop Wop (1908?)

I Trust My Husband Anywhere, But I Like to Stick Around (1909)

That's Yiddisha Love (1910)

Gee Whiz, Sweety! I'm Dead Stuck on You (1910)

Yum Pum Pa (1912)

My Hat's in the Ring (1912)

As Long as the Shamrock Grows Green (1912)

I Like It Better Every Day (1912)

In Dear Old Napoli (1915)

Down among the Sheltering Palms (1915)

The Story the Shamrock Told
(1915)

I Never Knew I Had a Heart
(1915)

The Silvery Man in the Silvery
Moon (1915)

America First (1916)

The Ghost of the Ukulele (1916)

Underneath the Weeping Willow
Tree (1916)

Why I Love You, I Don't Know
(1917)

In the Days of Old Black Joe
(1917)

Some Beautiful Morning (1917)

We're Going to Hang the Kaiser
under the Linden Tree (1917)

My Country—I Hear You Calling
Me (1917?)

I Miss Daddy's Good-Night Kiss
(1918)

Where It's Peach Jam Makin' Time
(1918)

The Greatest Little Mother in the
World (1918)

The Older They Get, the Harder
They Fall (1918)

Everybody's Happy Now (1918)

The Light That Shines Forever (Is
the Light at Home Sweet
Home) (1918)

We're Bound to Win with Boys
Like You (1918)

Palestine (1918)

Forget Me Not (1919)

I'm Forever Blowing Bubbles
(1919)

Golden Gate (1919)

I Know What It Means to Be
Lonesome (1919)

I Am Climbing Mountains (1919)

I'm Like a Ship without a Sail
(1919)

(It Seems Like) Ages and Ages
(1920)

Don't Blame It All on Me (1920)

It's All Right with Me, Old Pal
(1920)

Someone Took You Out of My
Arms (1920)

(All I Have Are) Sunny Weather
Friends (1920)

For Every Door That Closes,
Another Will Open for You
(1920)

Feather Your Nest (1920)

Once in a Blue Moon (1921)

Sunnyside Sal (1921)

When the Tide Comes In (1921)

Good as Gold (1921)

Jabberwocky (1921)

Bobbsey (1922)

You Darling You (1923)

Get Yourself a Broom and Sweep
Your Troubles Away (1924)

Oh! How I Wish I Knew (1924)

Nightingale (1924)

Silver Head (1925)

I Shouldn't Care But I Do (1925)

I Was Never So Lonesome Before
(1925)

Let's Grow Old Together (1926)

Wait Till My Ship Comes In (1926)

Laughing Eyes, Don't You Cry
(1926)

I Faw Down An' Go Boom! (1928)

Dream on a Piece of Wedding Cake
(1930)

I Wanna Be a Talking Picture
Queen (1930)

We'll Build a Little World of Our
Own (1930)

A Toast to the Girl I Love (1930)

Dough-Boy's Lullaby (1930)

Wrapped in a Red Red Rose (1930)

Put a Little Salt on the Bluebird's
Tail (1930)

Autumn Leaves*

Believe Me

Crickets in the Grass

Don't Forget Me
Ephram's Jazbo Band
Faithfully Yours
Garibaldi
Hample Pies
I Apologize*
Never You
Pich
Strumberry
Toodle-oo, I'll Be Seeing You
When the Last Rose of Summer
     Was in Bloom

Callaghan, Phebe Grant
Saginaw (1922)

Cherniavsky (Cherney), Josef
The Bells of Avalon (1927)
Love Sings a Song in My Heart
     (1929)
Today and Tomorrow (1929)
When You Were in Love with No
     One But Me (And I Was in
     Love with You) (1929)
Mississippi Misery (1937)
Some Other Time (1939?)
Her Heart Belongs to K. P. Jones
     (1942)
Hold Back the Dawn (1946?)
Eddy Band March (1952?)
We Fell in Love on Ojibway
     Island (1953)
Arnold
Dirt on the Downbeat
Drum of the Rhumba
Flying Jackass
Forever in Your Arms
If You Were Set to Music
Just Sweet
The Love Thief
Melody in Blue
Mother's Summer Parasol
Some Bright Tomorrow
Stars Look Down
Sweet Memories

Then and Now
You're First on Second Avenue

Cummins, Fred C. *See Hughes,*
Joseph H.

Fernett, Eugene "Gene"
It's Like Benny's
Mrs. Marks' Cha-Cha
Slightly Like the Duke
A Thousand Golden Horns
To Dorothy, With Love

Harris, Charles K.

When the Sun Has Set (1885)
Ah, There, Stay There
     (1885–1890)
Bake That Matzoh Pie
     (1885–1890)
I Hear Her Voice Again
     (1885–1890)
If I Were the Chief of Police
     (1885–1890)
Since Maggie Learned to Skate
     (1888)
Creep, Baby, Creep (1890)
Ma Black Tulip (1890)
I Used to Know Her Years Ago
     (1890)
Alderman Michael O'Rourke
     (1890?)
Sitting by the Kitchen Door
     (1890?)
Kiss and Let's Make Up (1891)
Hello, Central, Hello! (1891)
School Bells (When Baby Comes
     Home from School) (1891)
You'll Never Know (1891)
Thou Art Ever in My Thoughts
     (1891)
I Wonder, I Wonder* (1891)
Humming Baby to Sleep (1891)
Only a Tangle of Golden Curls
     (1891?)
Fallen by the Wayside (1892)

After the Ball (1892)

Can Hearts So Soon Forget? (1892)

I'm Trying So Hard to Forget You (1893)

Hearts (1893)

After Nine (1893)

Since Katie Rides a Wheel (1893)

Strangers (1893)

Is Life Worth Living? (1893)

I Love You in Spite of All (1893)

I Heard Her Voice Again (1894)

While the Dance Goes On (1894)

Cast Aside (1895)

There'll Come a Time (1895)

Better Than Gold (1895)

Just Behind the Times (1896)

I Love Her Just the Same (1896)

All for the Love of a Girl (1896)

Which Shall It Be? (1896)

Leonie, Queen of My Heart (1896)

The Organ-Grinder's Serenade (1897)

I've Just Come Back to Say Good-bye (1897)

Break the News to Mother (1897)

I've Been Faithful to You (1898)

'Mid the Green Fields of Virginia (1898)

Without Your Love, Ah Let Me Die! (1898)

There Is No Flag Like the Red, White and Blue (1898)

Dear College Chums (1898)

Ma Filipino Babe (1898)

Will I Find My Mamma There? (1898)

A Rabbi's Daughter (1899)

Just Tell Her That I Loved Her, Too (1899)

One Night in June (1899)

For Old Time's Sake (1900)

Do You Think You Could Learn to Love Me? (1900)

I've a Longing in My Heart for You, Louise (1900)

Just One Kiss (1900)

What Is a Home without Love? (1900)

Heart to Heart Waltzes (instrumental) (1900)

The Tie That Binds* (1901)

'Tis Not Always Bullets That Kill (1901)

In the Good Old Fashioned Way (1901)

Hello, Central, Give Me Heaven (1901)

Last Night As the Moon Was Shining (1901)

Must We Say Good-bye Forever Nellie Dear? (1901)

I'm Wearing My Heart Away for You (1902)

Just Next Door (1902)

In the Hills of Old Carolina (1902)

In Dear Old Fairy Land (1902)

Always in the Way (1903)

For Sale, a Baby (1903)

Just a Gleam of Heaven in Her Eyes (1903)

You Never Spoke to Me Like That Before (1903)

The Girl of My Dreams* (1903)

The Last Farewell (1903)

Down in the Vale of Shenandoah (1904)

Why Don't They Play with Me? (1904)

Love and Kisses (1904)

Farewell, Sweetheart May (1904)

On the Sands at Night (1904?)

Back to Life (1905)

Fly Away, Birdie, to Heaven (1905)

Charles K. Harris, *continued*

Dreaming, Love, of You (1905)

Would You Care? (1905)

Belle of the Ball* (1906)

And a Little Child Shall Lead Them (1906)

Somewhere* (1906)

Just Because I Loved You So (1907)

The Best Thing in Life (1907)

My Virginia (1907)

On Our Honeymoon (1907)

There's Another Picture in My Mamma's Frame (1907)

Yesterday* (1907)

It Might Have Been (1908)

I'm Starving for One Sight of You (1908)

A Man, A Maid, A Moon, A Boat (1908)

'Mid the Blue Grass of Kentucky (1909)

'Scuse Me Today (1909)

Was I a Fool? (1909)

Always Me (1909)

After 'While (1909)

Nobody Knows, Nobody Cares (1909)

In the City Where Nobody Cares (1910)

I Never Knew Till Now (1910)

I Want to Buy a Little Bit of Love (1910)

Don't Give Me Diamonds, All I Want Is You (1910)

It's Always June When You're in Love (1910)

Give Back My Sweetheart to Me (1911)

Don't Blame Me for Lovin' You (1911)

When the Golden Leaves Are Falling (1911)

I Miss You Honey, Miss You All the Time (1911)

Fairy Moon (1911)

Will the Roses Bloom in Heaven? (1911)

That Swaying Harmony (1911)

Climb a Tree with Me (1912)

Won't You Come to Dolly's Party? (1912)

Take Me in Your Arms Again (1912)

Tell Me a Beautiful Story (1912)

I Long for You Tonight (1912)

Not 'Till Then, Will I Cease to Love You (1912)

Love and Tears Waltzes (instrumental) (1912)

Don't You Wish You Were Back Home Again? (1913)

I'm Coming Back to You (1913)

No One Else Can Take Your Place (1913)

Suppose I Met You Face to Face (1913)

I Wonder Who's Next in Your Heart (1914)

When Angels Weep (Waltz of Peace) (1914)

When Did You Write to Mother Last? (1914)

Gee! But I'm So Awful Lonesome (1914)

Hooks and Eyes (1914)

You Kissed Me (instrumental) (1914)

The Lights of My Home Town (1915)

The Skating Waltzes (instrumental) (1915)

Can You Pay for a Broken Heart? (1915)

When It Strikes Home (1915)

My Mama Lives Up in the Sky (1915)

School Bells (Hear Them Ring) (1915)

Those Wonderful Words (I Love You) (1915)

Songs of Yesterday (1916)

All I Want Is a Cottage, Some Roses, and You (1916)

Come Back! (Let's Be Sweethearts Once More) (1916)

The Story of a Soul (1916)

A Study in Black and White (1917)

You Came, You Saw, You Conquered (1917)

Let Him Miss You Just a Little Bit (And He'll Think More of You) (1917)

Dry Your Tears (1917)

I'll See You Later, Yankee Land (1917)

Kathleen (My Rose) (1917)

Love O' Mine (1917)

Yankee (He's There, All There) (1917)

You Kissed Me (and Said Good-Bye) (1917)

What a Wonderful Dream It Would Be (1918)

Why Did You Come into My Life? (1918)

Will You Be There? (When I Come Back) (1918)

Is There a Letter for Me? (1918)

Will You Be True? (1918)

Smiling Lips (1919)

On a Little Side Street (1921)

Back Home and Broke (1922)

I Knew (1922?)

Danger in Your Eyes (1923?)

No One to Kiss You Good-Night (1924)

Without You (By My Side) (1924)

Iola (Pearl of the Southern Seas) (1924?)

Starlight, the Roses, and You (1929)

Dancing in a Dream (1930?)

Baby Hands

Baby's Eyes

Fifty Times a Day

He Was a Friend of Mine

Honey Boy, My Heart Is Calling for You

I Miss the Old Folks Now

Just a Bit of Driftwood on the Sea of Life

Mary Ann, Hollywood Is Calling You

Mississippi Twilight

Mud Pie Days

My Mother's Kiss (The Sweetest Kiss of All)

Please, Miss Central, Find My Mamma

Sweet Maid Devine

Then Comes the Sad Awakening

They Don't Want Me Back Home Again

Thou Shalt Not Steal a Heart Away

Voice of the Night Waltz (instrumental)

Waiting for Footsteps That Never Came

'Way Down Deep in My Heart

What Does the Flower Say?

When the Cherry Trees Are Blooming in Japan

Without a Wedding Ring

Hedrick, Jack

Adolf (1942)

Hughes, Joseph H.

Boys of the Winning Team (1909)

Come into That Dancing Crowd with Me (1914)

I'm Going Back to That Old Town (1914)

Ireland, Dear Ireland (1914)

You're the Girl for Me (1914)

When You Gave the World to Me (1916)

I Long to See Ireland Once More (1918)

Hughes, Joseph H., with Fred C. Cummins (Cummings)

Would You Like to Take a Walk with Me? (1908)

Love Me Dearly (1910)

Take a Ride on a Steamboat (1910)

If I Were Only Loved by You (1910)

I Love the Name of Erin (1913)

O You Angel with the Dreamy Eyes (1913)

That Irish Ragtime Bear (1913)

I Love You with Your Merry Widow Hat

Hughes, Joseph H., with Harry Richardson

Mother O' Mine (1914)

The Finest Flag That Flies (1914)

When Shadows of Evening Are Falling (I Miss You Most of All) (1914)

You're My Little Playmate (1914)

Since I Lost You, Mother O' Mine (1915)

You're the Star I Love Best (1915)

I'll Anchor My Ship in Your Harbor of Love (1915)

J. Warren Kerrigan (The Hero of Them All) (1915)

Where the Nightingale Woos the Rose (1916)

How Would You Like to Have a Loving Boy Like Me? (1917)

One Gladsome Day (1917)

I'll Come Marching Back to You (1918)

Jones, Isham

Midsummer Evenings (1906)

Soldiers of the Sea (instrumental) (1912)

In My Canoe (1913)

(At That) Dixie Jubilee (1915)

Say, Young Feller, Where'd You Get That Girl? (1918)

Indigo Blues (1918)

Meet Me in Bubble Land (1918)

He's a Darn Good Man to Have Hanging Around (1919)

I'm the Ghost of an Old Time Melody (1920)

Sweet Woman (1920)

There's No Better Time Than Now (1920)

When Shadows Fall, I Hear You Calling, California (1920)

Wishing (1920)

What'll You Do? (1921)

Broken Hearted Melody (1922)

Ivy (Cling to Me) (1922)

On the Alamo (1922)

Pipe Organ Blues (1922)

Play the Funny Blues (1922)

Pilgrim's Blues (instrumental) (1922?)

Samson and Delilah (instrumental) (1922?)

All Wrong (1923)

Indiana Moon (1923)

Kaintucky (1923)

Shanghai Lullaby (1923)

Swingin' Down the Lane (1923)

What Could Be Sweeter (1923)

At the End of a Winding Lane (1924)

Gotta Getta Girl (1924)

I'll See You in My Dreams (1924)

Insufficient Sweetie (1924)

Some Other Day—Some Other Girl (1924)

I Want to Be Left Alone (1924)

Never Again (1924)

It Had to Be You (1924)

Spain (1924)

The One I Love Belongs to Somebody Else (1924)

Where Is That Old Girl of Mine? (1924)

Why Couldn't It Be Poor Little Me? (1924)

Ida I Do (1925)

I'm Tired of Everything But You (1925)

Headin' for Home (1925)

Lady of the Nile (1925)

My Castle in Spain (1925)

Gone Again Gal (1926)

Nobody's Gonna Keep Me Away from My Girl (1926)

The Cat (1927)

If You See Sally (1927)

One More Kiss (and Then Goodbye) (1927)

Pleading (1927)

The Spell o' the Moon (1927)

Down Where the Sun Goes Down (1928)

The Hour of Parting (orchestration) (1928)

There's Somebody New (1928)

Feelin' That Way (1929)

Song of the Blues (1929)

You're Not the Same Old Girl (1929)

I Keep Remembering Someone I Should Forget (1930)

What's the Use? (1930)

I Wouldn't Change You for the World (1931)

My Cradle Sweetheart (1931)

You're Just a Dream Come True (1931)

I Can't Believe It's True (1932)

If You Were Only Mine (1932)

I'll Never Have to Dream Again (1932)

I Only Found You for Somebody Else (1932)

Let's Try Again (1932)

Let That Be a Lesson to You (1932)

One Little Word Led to Another (1932)

Second Hand Heart for Sale (1932)

The Wooden Soldier and the China Doll (1932)

All Mine (Almost) (1933)

Honestly (1933)

No More, No Less (1933)

Old Lace (1933)

Something Seems to Tell Me (1933)

There's Nothing Left to Do But Say Goodbye (1933)

Tick Tock Town (1933)

Why Can't This Night Go on Forever? (1933)

You've Got Me Crying Again (1933)

Bubbles in the Wine* (1934)

Don't Cry, Baby (1934)

How Strange (1934)

It's Funny to Everyone but Me (1934)

Romance in the Rain (1934)

The Waltz of Love (1934)

You're Welcome (1934)

Give a Broken Heart a Break (1935)

Midnight Rendezvous (1935)

Where the Rocky Mountains Kiss the Sky (1935)

Let Me Be the One in Your Heart (1936)

There Is No Greater Love (1936)

Just to Remind You (1937)

Thanks for Everything (1937)

More Than Ever (1938)

Go 'Way (Can't You See I'm Dreaming?) (1940)

But I Never Do (1942)

Just to Be Near You (1942)

My Best to You (1942)

With No Man of My Own (1942)

How Many Tears Must Fall? (1948)

Melinda (1951)

Sally Doesn't Care (1951)

Barefoot Boy of Mine

The Batoneer March

Foo

The General's House
I Got into the Wrong Dream
I'll Be Faithful
It Ain't What You Want
Jones' Melody
Just Like You
Main Event March
Marching Home with the Dawn
Mary, I'm in Love with You
Mein Fruehling Bist Du
Midnight Serenade
Nickels and Quarters and Dimes
Not a Cloud in the Sky
Now or Never*
Now the Whole World Knows
Out of the Blue Sky
Piccolo Polka
Salute to Sousa
She Picked It Up in Mexico
Too Good for My Own Good
The Trojan
When I Look at You
You Didn't Have to Tell Me
Yvette

Jones, Isham, with Gerald Marks

If We Should Never Meet Again
(1934)

Jones, Isham, with Olaf "Ole" W. Olsen

Back to Georgia Bay (1916)
Frisco's Chinatown (1916)
That's Gay (1916)
Cremona Man (1916)
America Won't You Take Me Back
to You (1917)
That's Jaz (1917)
We're in the Army Now* (1917)
Call for Mister Brown (1918)
Oh! Min! (1918)
There's One More River We're
Going to Cross (and That's
the River Rhine) (1918)

Knodel, Dorothy L. *See Wheeler, Susaine P.*

Kremer, Walter F.

Those Were the Days (1929)
Around the Town (March)

Lorenzo, Ange

Come Down to Tennessee (1915)
Dreamy Dream Girl (1915)
Aladdin's Bungalow (1916)
Listen in on Lester (1922)
Sleepy Time Gal (1925)
I've Waited for This (1926)
Sweet Forget-Me-Not (1928)
Rainy Days (1931)
Watching for Your Shadow (1937)
Jean*
My Boy Friend Stole My Girl
Friend

Lorenzo, Ange, with Howard "Howdy" Quicksell

I Want the Girl of My Dreams to
Be the Girl in My Arms
(1947)

MacGregor, John Chalmers "Chummy"

Doin' the Jive (1937)
Sold American (1939)
Slumber Song (1941)
It Must Be Jelly ('Cause Jam
Don't Shake Like That)
(1942)
It's Lovin' Time (1946)
A Little Bit Longer (1947)
Get Me to Kansas City
I Sustain the Wings
Mr. Lucky Me*
Moon Dreams
Saturday Night Mood
Simply Grand
Why Don't We Say We're Sorry?

Marienthal, Paul. *See Williams, Lewis J.*

Marks, Gerald

Little Redheaded Boy (1925)

Everybody Has Someone But Me
(1925)

She's Drivin' Me Wild (1925)

Nobody Worries 'Bout Me (1926)

Gee! I'm Glad I Found a Girl
Like You (1926)

Where in the World (Is There
Someone for Me?) (1927)

I'd Walk a Million Miles (to Be a
Little Bit Nearer to You)
(1927)

A Lane in Spain (1927?)

Gonna Get a Girl (1927?)

Give Me a Day in June (1927?)

Slue Foot (1927?)

Sweet Child (1927?)

As Long As I Live (1928)

Nothin' to Do but Love (1931)

(With You on My Mind, I Find) I
Can't Write the Words (1931)

All of Me (1931)

You're the One, You Beautiful
Son-of-a-Gun (1931)

I'll Get Along Somehow (1931)

How Can I Be Anything But
Blue? (1931)

I Walked Out on All the Other
Girls (1931)

I'm Grateful (1931)

That's Heaven to Me (1931)

Little Mama Doll (1931)

Anywhere with You (1931)

Can't You Hear That Bluebird?
(1931)

Every Time My Heart Beats
(1932))

The Night Shall Be Filled with
Music (1932)

When I Look into Your Eyes
(1932)

Save a Rainy Day for Me (1932)

I'll Be Much Obliged to You
(1932)

I'll See You in the Morning
(1932)

I'm So in Love with You (1932)

Molly and Me (1932)

Who Do You Love, Baby? (1932)

Am I In, Am I Out? (1932)

Why Am I Afraid of You? (1932)

Honolulu Lady (1932)

You Are the Whole Parade (1932)

For All You Care (1932)

Fond Recollections, Mem'ries of
Old (1933)

It Was a Summer Serenade (1933)

Let's Spend an Evening at Home
(1933)

Say What You Mean and Mean
What You're Saying to Me
(1933)

The Sun Is Shining for My Baby
and Me (1933)

Back Home (1933)

Now We're on Our Second
Honeymoon (1933)

Bohemia (1933)

Ask Your Heart (1933)

Dream On (1933)

I Can Sew a Button (1933)

Moody and Blue (1933)

My International Girl (1933)

'Till Doomsday (1933)

Once in a While* (1933)

Nothing But the Best (1933)

Oh You, You Beautiful Thing
(1933)

Reunion in Reo (1934)

They Ought to Give a Letter to
Mabel (1934)

Come on and Do Your Hallelujah,
Now (1934)

Have You Ever Been in Love?
(1934)

I Don't Know What to Make of
You (1934)

Gerald Marks, continued

Poor Girl (1934)

Trav'lling the Road (1934)

Cubanola Rumbanette (1934)

Here Comes the Captain (1934)

Without a Shirt (1934)

Malibu (1934)

Sailing on the Night Boat, Where the Hudson Flows (1935)

Soldier of Love (1935)

Oh, Suzanna, Dust Off That Old Piana (1935)

Forbidden Melody (1935)

Let Your Heart Make up Your Mind (1935)

I'm a Fugitive from a Chain Letter Gang (1935)

I Don't Know Your Name But You're Beautiful (1935)

That's What I Want for Christmas (1935)

The Man Who Makes the Gun (1935)

The Rooster's Crowin' (Cock-a-Doodle-Do) (1936)

Is It True What They Say about Dixie? (1936)

All Quiet on the Front Porch Tonight (1936)

The First Rose of Summer (The Last Rose of My Heart) (1936)

Would 'Ja Have a Cup O' Java with Me? (1936)

I Want the Whole World to Love You (1936)

I Would Love to Have You Love Me (1936)

Saskatchewan (1936)

Breakfast in Harlem (1936)

Spanish Jake (1936)

I Don't Sleep at Night But Oh I Dream All Day (1936)

There Must Be a Heaven for That Little Dog of Mine (1936)

I Believe Every Word I've Heard about You (1936)

Donald Duck (1936)

The Door Is Open Again (1937)

My Spies Tell Me (You Love Nobody But Me) (1937)

I Think You're Ducky (1937)

Ev'ryone's Out So Let's Stay in Tonight (1937)

First, Last, and Always (1937)

I Love to Sing the Words While We're Dancing (1938)

Faster, Faster, My Heart Is Breaking (1938)

Goodnight, Molly O'Day (1938)

Oh, What a Day That Will Be (1938)

Mary the Milkman's Daughter (1938)

I'm Through Throwing Good Love After Bad (1939)

Cuba-Duba-Do (1939)

A Ruble a Rhumba (1939)

No More (1939)

If It's Good, Then I Want It (1939)

The G. T. Stomp (1939)

Kick It (1939)

The Silver Lining* (1939)

There's the Devil to Pay (1939)

It's the Things You Do with Your Feet (1939)

Me and Columbus (1939)

Baby, What Else Can I Do? (1939)

Waltz in Blue (1939)

The Timbuctoo (1939)

Love Is Such a Cheat (1939)

I've Got Two Left Feet (1940)

Put the Swanee Up in Bottles and Send It Up to Me (1940)

The Name Song (1940)

Ev'ryone's a Fighting Son of That Old Gang of Mine (1940)

Dancing Silhouette (1940)

Magnolias and Moonbeams (1940)

The Man Is Solid (1940)

Bow, Wow, Wow, Wow, Wow (1940)

What Would I Do Without You (1940)

For a Good Game of Marbles (1940)

Hooray, Hooray for Nancy Mix (1940)

I Toot a Big Toot on My Horn (1940)

Pipes of Pan-Americana (1940)

When You Tend Baby (1940)

Driving on Monday or Tuesday or Sunday (1940)

I've Got a Date with a Bond (1941)

Remember Pearl Harbor* (1941)

We Won't Let You Down, Old England (1941)

When You Hear the Sirens Blow (1941)

The Elevator Man (1941)

Be Good to Soldiers While Your Daddy's Away (1942)

Here Comes That Moon Again (1942)

Dig Down Deep (1942)

The Pied Piper (of Hamlin Town) (1942)

With a Forty Dollar Buggy and a Twenty Dollar Horse (1942)

The News Is Good, the News Is Bad (1942)

Lazy Mary* (1942)

Shake Hands with Your Air-Raid Warden (1942)

Walk with Uncle Sam (1942)

Don't Let a Blackout Give You a Knockout (1942)

The Traffic That Roars in the Spring (1942)

Soldiers of Home Defense (1942)

Feet on the Sidewalk (Head in the Sky) (1943)

Now That I'm Free (1943)

One Pair of Pants for You (1943)

You Who Go Driving for Pleasure (1943)

If You Like Bananas (1943)

Date in Dixie (1943)

Dear Son of Mine, My Little Lad (1943)

Father in That Factory (1943)

Etiquette in the Zoo (1943)

Good News, Bad News (1943)

I Care for You, You Care for Me (1943)

One for You and Two for Uncle Sam (1943)

When Roses Are Red and Eyelids Are Blue (1943)

Victory Pie (1943)

Rub A Dub Dub, I've Had a Good Scrub (1943)

Adolf and Benito (1943)

Factory Whistles Are Bugles to Me (1943)

If You Want to Be an Edison (1943)

Johnny Be Careful (1943)

A Patriotic Family Are We (1943)

Rain on the Sea (1943)

There Ain't No Color Line around the Rainbow (1943)

This Is Our Private Love Song (1943)

Hitch Your Wagon to 48 Stars (1943)

Don't Leave Banana Peels on the Street (1943)

At the World's Fair (1943)

Meet Miss Victory (1943)

Good Lookin' (It's Good Lookin' at You) (1944)

A Million Dollars Worth of Sunshine (1944)

Gerald Marks, continued

When a World That's Been So Wrong So Long (1945)

Ladies, Ladies (1945)

Among the Daisies (1945)

The Church Bells Are Ringing for Mary (But Not for Mary and Me) (1945)

Ev'ryone Is Looking for the Rainbow (1945)

Mountain Gal (1945)

Since Lum Come Hum (1945)

Where'd You Get Those Clothes? (1945)

Could You Be True? (1945)

I Wish I Had Died at the Altar (1945)

The Perfect March (1945)

I Was Only Foolin' (1945)

Cut the Knot—Turn Me Loose—Set Me Free (1946)

You Can Wait Beneath That Apple Tree (1946)

Lelia's Horsie (1947)

Two and Two Are One (1947)

The Dodger's Song (1947)

Never More (1948)

It Was So Nice Having You (1948)

Hold It (1948)

Down the Well (1948)

Buck in the Bank (1948)

Always You (1948)

About Face (1948)

Friendly Enemy (1948)

You Took Possession of Me (1948)

Heaven Sent (1948)

Fundamental Character (1948)

Roll 'Em* (1948)

Courage (1948)

Everyone Loves a Holiday (1948)

Our Anniversary (1949)

Chummy (1949)

The Carousel Song* (1949)

The Roller Coaster Song (1949)

Good Morning, Teacher (1949)

Ti-Yi, Yippee! (1949)

If It Doesn't Snow on Christmas (1949)

A Schmoo Can Do Most Anything (1949)

The Broken Down Town of Dogpatch (1949)

The Schmoo Doesn't Cost a Thing (1949)

Snuggable, Huggable Schmoo (1949)

Schmoo Music (1949)

The Schmoo Club (1949)

The Schmoo Is Clean, the Schmoo Is Neat (1949)

There Never Was a Place Like Saginaw (1949)

Welcome to My Heart (1950)

Snow White and the Seven Dwarfs (1950)

The Little Rag Doll with the Shoe Button Eyes (1950)

Bucky, the Bucking Bronco (1950)

Vot Giffs Mit Der Dictionary? (1950)

It Was Good Enough for My Father (So It's Good Enough for Me) (1950)

The Guy That I Send to Congress (1950)

Fifty Years Ago (1950)

Let's All Shed a Tear (1950)

Election Day (1950)

It Can Only Happen in the U.S.A. (1950)

Guffy, the Goofy Gobbler (1950)

The Wobblin' Goblin (with the Broken Broom) (1950)

I Don't Want a Lot for Christmas
    (1950)
Frosty Mornin' (1950)
Labor Day (1950)
On a Picket Line (1950)
First Day at School (1950)
When Everything Tastes Like Ice
    Cream (1950)
Krausmeyer's Band (1951)
My Choc'late Rabbit (1951)
Vas You Ever in Cincinatti?
    (1951)
The Little Engine That Could
    (1951)
If You Don't Marry Me (1951)
I Met an Old Friend of Yours
    (1951)
Who's Excited? (1951)
Alice in Wonderland (1951)
Lead a Little Orchestra (1951)
The Witch of Salem (1952)
My Home Town (1952)
Hansel and Gretel* (1952)
If God Can Forgive Me, Why
    Can't You? (1952)
Two Little Roses (1952)
I'd Rather Forgive You Than
    Forget You (1953)
Hello Summer, Where You Been
    All Winter? (1953)
I'll Cry Tomorrow (1953)
Weary I (1954)
The Lucky Little Bell of San
    Michele (1954)
It's a Wonderful Thing to Be
    Loved (1954)
To My Mother on My Birthday
    (1954)
What Shall We Sing about
    America? (1955)
What Is Brotherhood Week?
    (1955)
Give Me Your Hand
Vote for the Mayor for Mayor

*Although Tin Pan Alley had lost
    much of its influence on
    American entertainment by the
    late 1950s, Marks continued to
    write songs in what could be con-
    sidered a Tin Pan Alley style for
    some years afterward. Some of
    these songs are listed below.*

Is Your Name in the Book?
    (1956)
Don't Torture Me (1956)
A Guy and His Gal (1956)
When You Reach the Age of 21
    (1956)
Come to the Aid of Your Party
    (1958)
Who Wants Love? (1958)
Time (1959)
Genevieve* (1960)
Let Me Grow Lovely, Growing
    Old (1960)
Wherever You Are Today (1963)
The Grouchy Gaucho (1963)
RSVP (1963)
Strengthen the Arm of Liberty
    (1963)
Always a Bridesmaid But Never a
    Bride (1965)
The Lord Will Always Meet You
    Half Way (1965)
April Snow (1965)
Build a World of Love (1966)
Hail to His Honor the Mayor
    (1966)
One Broken Dream Is Not the
    End of Dreaming (1966)
Life Is a Prayer (1967)
Time (1967)
I Want Music All My Life (1986?)

Marks, Gerald, with Isham Jones.
    *See Jones, Isham, with Gerald
    Marks*

McWatters, Arthur J.

The Girl Whom We All Admire
(1896)
Bess, My Bess (1896)
The Society Belle (1897)
Hearts or Diamonds (1899)
Without Thee, Dear Heart (1900)
Call Me Darling
Delilah Waltz
My Alabama Lady
My Lily Queen
Now You Think You're Awful
Smart
Oh, Child of Mine
We'll Meet Again*
You're the Girl I Love

Mikolaizyk, Irene Turnbull M.

There's a Ring Around My Finger
(and a Glow Around My
Heart) (1945)

Miller, Ernest

How Could I Be Blue? (1930)
Where the Roses Are So Beautiful
(There's a Home for You and
Me) (1932)

Nauer, John B.

The Aussies and the Yanks Are
Here (1942)
Say a Prayer (1943)
I Found a Princess in Queensland
(1943)
Fuzzy Wuzzy Angels (1943)

Northrup, Blanche

Take Me Back to Home Sweet
Home (1921)

Olsen, Olaf "Ole" W. *See also Jones,
Isham, with Olaf "Ole" W. Olsen*

When Will the War Be Over?
(1943)

Patton, Elmer G.

California Blues (1923?)
Some Little Someone (1928)
Stolen Moments (1930)

Picard, Frank. *See also Russo,
Danny, with Frank Picard*

My Girl at Michigan (1911)
That Tantalizing Strain (1918)
Girl of My Smoke Wreaths (1918)
We're Ready to Go, Say the Word
(1918)
That's Not for Me (1918)
Don't Worry, Little Girl (1918)
I Wouldn't Throw the Khaki
Down, Would You? (1918)
The Song of the 85th (1918)
The Loveliest Girl on Earth
(1918)
I Need Someone Just Like You
(1918)
I'd Like to Be Young Again
(1918)
When They Build That Dixie
Highway (1918)
C-O-L-U-M-B-U-S
The Girls with the New Idear

Quicksell, Howard "Howdy." *See
also Lorenzo, Ange, with Howard
Quicksell*

You Are Just a Vision (1925)
Since My Best Girl Turned Me
Down (1927)
Sorry (1927)
The Way I Feel Today (1929)
Pardon the Glove

Richardson, Harry. *See Hughes,
Joseph H., with Harry
Richardson*

Robinson, Jack

Sunshine Valley (1937)
Gee, I Wish I Was Rich (1949)

Roeser, Harold, with Archie Zander

Teasing Me (1946)

Rupp, Carl

Arizona Stars (1923)
Lovely Lady (1924)
Tonight's the Night (1924)
Footloose (1925)
The Flapper Wife (1925)
Can You Imagine That (1926)
Just an Ivy Covered Shack (1926)
Love Bound (1926)
Baby-Mine (1927)
'Tho You Threw Me Down (1928)
The Black Pigeon Wing (1929)
Michigan Marches On (1937)
Don't Bother Me
Early in the Morning
I Feel So Good
Isn't It Wonderful
Lost Word Melody (Into My Arms Dear)
Love Bound
My Sweetie and Me
My Tango Girl
The Rickety Rackety Shack
When You Come to the End of Your Dreams
Who Could Ask for More?

Russo, Danny

Toot, Toot, Tootsie, Goo'Bye (1921)
California Rose (1922)
Oriole Blues (1922)
Old Kentucky Blues (1923)
Back in Hackensack New Jersey (1924)
Moonlight and You (1924)
Ukelele Lady (1925)
Wouldn't It Be Wonderful? (1929)

Because of You*
I Couldn't Help It if I Tried
Imagination*
Isabelle
Lost
My Dream Moon
Night
Oh, Lizzie
Roses
Tonight*

Russo, Danny, with Frank Picard

It Comes from I-ta-lee (1915)

Vervoort, Clara

'Cause I'm Idiotic Over You (1940)

Volz, Sallie Logan

Keep in Step (1942)

Way, Mary Frances

It Was Nice to Have Known You (1937)
It's a Man's World (1947)

Weisman, Ben

Makes a Difference to My Heart (1947)
You Are My Love (1947)
How Do You Measure Love? (1947)
Once More (1949)
The Way You Shake Your Maracas (1949)
Have a Little Sympathy (1949)
Mambo Jive (1950)
What Happened? (1950)
I Wish I Were a Kid This Christmas (1950)
You Know You Did, You Know You Did (1950)
Heartbreak Hill (1951)
Winky Dink (1951)

Ben Weisman, continued

I Don't Believe in Tomorrow (1951)
Oklahoma Polka (1951)
I'll R'ar Back and Kiss You (1951)
Blue River Blues (1951)
Oh It Feels So Good (1951)
Momma Won't You Teach Me? (1951)
Rollicka Polka (1951)
Gentle Johnny (1952)
You'll Never Be Mine (1952)
Never Let Her Go (1952)
Strange Sensation (1952)
The Family That Prays Together Is the Family That Stays Together (1952)
The Wallflower Waltz (1952)
Don't Build Your Dreams Too High (1952)
Won't You Surrender (1952)
The Magic Violin (1952)
Drums of Desire (1952)
Paper Roses (1952)
Blue River Valley (1952)
What Can You Do with a Lazy Woman? (1952)
You Put a Spell on Me (1952)
Rosey Red Cheeks (1952)
The Bugabooboo (1952)
Mississippi Cattle Boat (1952)
Beautiful Words of Love (1952)
Come to the Ball (1952)
No One to Call Your Own (1952)
I Want the World to Know (1952)
I Leave My Heart with You (1952)
Shaun, Shaun the Leprechaun (1952)
Angel on the Battlefield (1952)
Pretty Black Eyed Susie (1953)
Oo What You Do to Me* (1953)
Mother Nature and Father Time (1953)

Honey in the Horn (1953)
Let's Walk Thataway (1953)
You're on Trial (1953)
My Bunny and My Sister Sue (1953)
Satisfaction Guaranteed (1953)
Golden Violins (1953)
Sweet Thing (1953)
The Coronation Waltz (1953)
Every Prayer Is a Flower (in the Garden of the Lord) (1953)
Who'll Buy My Heartaches? (1953)
The First Time I Told You a Lie (1953)
Easy Pickins (1953)
The Blueberry Boy (With the Strawberry Hair) (1953)
The Night I Ran Away (1953)
Pueblo Pipe Pow Wow (1953)
The Song of a Broken Heart (1953)
Sawdust on the Floor (1953)
Take Your Time Boy (1953)
Life Is Worth Living (1953)
You Made Me Purr (1953)
When Love Comes Knocking at Your Door (1953)
Tango (1953)
Trinidaddy (1953)
Slender Tender and Sweet (1953)
An Old Fashioned Wedding (1953)
My Sentimental Sweetheart (1953)
Forgotten Forlorn and Forsaken (1953)
Dead Man's Guitar (1953)
Rock Bottom Blues (1953)
Dance Till Your Heart Breaks (1953)
Mississippi (1953)
Nightingale Nocturne (1953)
Jenny Jenkins (1953)

Have Mercy (1953)
Somebody's Moving In (1953)
The Silver Bells of Memory (1953)
Everyone Kissed the Bride but Me (1953)
Heartbreak Train (1953)
Waltz of the Autumn Leaves (1953)
When a Woman Loves a Man* (1953)
Who Knows (1953)
No Now (1953)
Blue Bayou Moon (1953)
Give Me More (1953)
Chu Chu the Chocolate Chick (1953)
Babunda (1953)
Jungle Rain (1953)
An Old Country Custom (1953)
Soft Violins on a Rainy Night (1953)
Love Isn't Love (1953)
Your Kiss (1953)
Two in the Middle (1953)
You Gotta Be Good to Me (1953)
Tapioca (1953)
I Can't Help Thinking of You (1953)
The Little General (1953)
Cuckoo Clock Boogie (1953)
You Will Be Heard (1953)
I Just Wanna Get Away (1953)
Broadway Will Be Hallelujah Street (When the Boys Come Home Again) (1953)
Plantation Love (1953)
Teenage Love (1953)
I Was Saved (1953)
Now That I Care (1953)
Forbidden Fruit (1953)
My Heart Has Many Dreams (1953)
The Corn Stalk Fiddle (With the Shoe String Bow) (1953)

Laredo Waltz (1953)
Theme (1953)
Bamboula (1953)
Sweet Papaya (1953)
Low Down High Land Swing (1953)
Honey Babe (1953)
If All My Tears Were Pearls (1953)
Prince Charming (1953)
Half Way to Heaven (1953)
Mandolino (1953)
Starlight Serenade (1954)
La Lupa (1954)
Double Datin' (1954)
The Rosary of Roses (1954)
Double Crossed by Love (1954)
From Nine to Five* (1954)
In the Beginning (1954)
I'll Meet You Coming Down the Ladder (1954)
Seeds of Jealousy (1954)
Steady Diet (1954)
My Daddy Has Two Sweethearts (1954)
Where the Rolling Mountains Meet the Rolling Sea (1954)
Gerald McBoing Boing (1954)
When the World Turns Its Back on You (1954)
The Army of the Lord (1954)
(I'm Only as Strong as) Your Love for Me (1954)
Moo Goo Gai Pan (1954)
Guilty Lips (1954)
Someone Ate My Apple (1954)
This Night Will Go On Forever (1954)
Rig-a-jig-a-jack (1954)
It's Wonderful to Be Loved (1954)
I'm a One O'Clock Gal (in a Nine O'Clock Town) (1954)
My Love (1954)

Ben Weisman, continued

Beware (1954)
God's Country and Mine (1954)
(The Flag of My Country and)
    the Banner of the Lord (1954)
Cry My Heart (1954)
Cool* (1954)
The Heart of a Fool (1954)
The Bride and Groom Mambo
    (1954)
Christmas Kisses (1954)
Time Changes Everything (1954)
May Your Life Be a Song (1954)
My Sin Is You (1954)
The Penalty of Love (1954)
You're Part of Me (1954)
Let Me Be Free (1954)
My Brother's Keeper (1955)
Oh Yeah (1955)
The Miracle of Love (1955)
Billy Bubble Gum (1955)
Mi Muchacha (1955)

The Tin Pan Alley years ended about 1955, but Weisman continued to write popular songs for many years after that—some in the style of Tin Pan Alley, and some in other styles. Many are listed below.

Tiger Lily (I Love Her So) (1956)
Lonely Winter (1956)
First in Line (1956)
Over and Over Again (1956)
The Christmas Blues (1956)
Paper Castles (1956)
Is It Only That You're Lonely?
    (1956)
Please, Don't Do That to Me
    (1956)
Where You Are (There I Want to
    Be) (1956)
Open Up Your Heart (and Let
    Me In) (1956)

Unconditional Surrender (1956)
Ever Since I Can Remember
    (1956)
Jimmy Jimmy (1956)
Moonlight Swim (1957)
Don't Leave Me Now (1957)
Sweet Stuff (1957)
Don't You Worry Your Pretty
    Little Head (1957)
Got a Lot of Livin' to Do (1957)
Third Finger Left Hand (1957)
C'mon, Let's Go (1957)
Warmed Over Kisses—Left Over
    Love (1957)
I Can't Close the Book (1957)
It Takes Only One (1957)
Is It Only When You're Lonely?
    (1957)
That's Why a Steel Guitar Cries
    (1957)
That's What I Learned in School
    (1957)
Teenage Wedding (1957)
Heartbreak Lane (1957)
If Ya Don't Like It, Don't Knock
    It (1957)
Playin' Possum (1957)
If Any Man Loves You More
    (1957)
Miracle Man (1957)
(You Make Me Do It) Every Time
    (1957)
Nobody Understands Me (1957)
Pick Another Baby (1957)
Hungry Eyes (1957)
Jamboree (1957)
Symphony of Love (1957)
Coming from You (1958)
Crawfish (1958)
Scotch on the Rocks (1958)
When I Am with You (1958)
Don't Ask Me Why (1958)
School of Love (1958)
Lend Me Your Comb (1958)
Lonely Blue Boy (Danny) (1958)
Tears after Midnight (1958)

Lady Bug (1958)

Every Little Once in a While (1958)

Annie Oakley* (1958)

Baby, Take Me Back (1958)

Like Wow (1958)

The School of Love (1958)

Double Dutch (1958)

A Still Small Voice (1958)

Torn Between Two Loves* (1958)

As Long As I Have You (1958)

That Girl Next Door* (1958)

The Headhunters (1958)

Under a Rainbow (and over the Blues) (1958)

It's Easy to Say You're Sorry (1958)

Dangerous Doll (1958)

See You Around (1958)

One Thing Led to Another (1958)

I'm Breaking in a Broken Heart (1959)

Rock, Little Chillun! (1959)

Run, Rabbit, Run (1959)

Playin' the Field (1959)

That's All I'm Living For (1959)

I Want That (1959)

I'm Willing to Learn (1959)

Nowhere to Go (1959)

The Journey (1959)

Make Believe Baby (1959)

A Lover's Prayer (1959)

Head Shoulder Baby (1959)

Talking Pictures (1959)

Silent Movies (1959)

Got a Letter from Mama (1959)

I Like Girls (1959)

Bye Bye Lulu (1959)

What Difference Does It Make (1959)

Alibi (1959)

Face to Face (1960)

The Hurt in My Heart (1960)

Fame and Fortune (1960)

Let Me Know (1960)

Is It Better to Have Loved and Lost? (1960)

Try Me (1960)

It Feels So Right (1960)

I Hope I Never Wake Up (1960)

If There's Ever a Next Time (1960)

Crazy Night (1960)

Standing By (1960)

Now's the Time (1960)

Pocketfull of Rainbows (1960)

A Miracle Happened to Me (It Could Happen to You) (1960)

Engaged to You (1960)

(You Don't Have a) Wooden Heart (1960)

Especially for the Young (1960)

Movin' Away (1960)

I Go Down to the River (1961)

In My Way (1961)

I Slipped, I Stumbled, I Fell (1961)

Summer Kisses, Winter Tears (1961)

Don't Make Me Love You (1961)

You're Wonderful and You're Mine (1961)

Till There Were None (1961)

Too Big for Her Bikini (1961)

Beach Boy (1961)

I Too Have No Wooden Heart (1961)

Almost Always True (1961)

Rockahula Baby (1961)

Oh Happiness (1961)

Bridge of Love (1961)

Springfield (1961)

Christmas Blues (1961)

Dick Tracy (1961)

A Kiss for Christmas (1961)

Little Dolly (1962)

Follow That Dream (1962)

Stepping Out of Line (1962)

Ben Weisman, *continued*

It Won't Be Me (1962)
This Is Living (1962)
Riding the Rainbow (1962)
I Got Lucky (1962)
My Christmas Love (1962)
The Night Has a Thousand Eyes
  (1962)
Limbo with Me (1963)
Happy Ending (1963)
Beyond the Bend (1963)
This Is Where I Came In (1963)
If She Doesn't Want You (1963)
A Great Night for Crying (1963)
No More (1963)
Fun in Acapulco (1963)
Christmas Star (1963)
What Can I Give Him (1963)
Slowly but Surely (1963)
Livin' High (1963)
Margarita (1964)
Everything I Need (1964)
I'll Touch a Star (1864)
For You My Love (1964)
Playing with Fire (1964)
The Leaves Will Fall (1964)
Fortune Smiled at Me (1964)
Face in the Shadow (1964)
It's Carnival Time (1964)
Moon Maid (1965)
Never Trust a Stranger (1965)
Do the Clam (1965)
A Voice in the Wind (1965)
The Young Americans (1965)
Away from the Crowd (1965)
Summer (1965)
Johnny Turn Your Head Away
  (1965)
Show Me the Way (1965)
Turn Around (1965)
The Thrill of Lovin' You (1965)
Forget Me Never (1965)
Gotta Get Away (1965)
Got a Feeling (1965)
Make Me Happy (1965)

The Sword and Dragon (1965)
Wild Love (1965)
Big Boy (1965)
Someone's Crying (1965)
It's Happening (1965)
Mail Call (1966)
It's All in Your Mind (1966)
Frankie & Johnny (arrangement
  of an old ballad) (1966)
Chesay (1966)
Hard Luck (1966)
Secret Island (1966)
A Dog's Life (1966)
You Only Think of Me (1966)
All I See Is You (1966)
Spinout (1966)
I'll Be Back (1966)
Blue Lou* (1966)
So Close to Love (1966)
Chicken Walk (1966)
Back Street (1966)
Yoga Baby (1966)
Bah-Zoom (1966)
Now More Than Ever (1966)
Don't Let Me Down (1966)
This Too Shall Pass (1966)
Easy Come, Easy Go (1967)
Mister Sunshine (1967)
Hollywood Wheels (1967)
It Won't Be Long (1967)
There Is So Much World to See
  (1967)
How Can You Lose (1967)
Clambake (1967)
He's Your Uncle, Not Your Dad
  (1967)
Who Am I (1967)
Somebody (1967)
Stay Away Joe (1967)
Dominic (1967)
All I Needed Was the Rain (1967)
We Call on Him (1968)
Broken Guitar (1968)
Who Are You (Who Am I)
  (1968)

That's What I Call Christmas
   (1968)
Somehow (1968)
Autumn Sings a Sad, Sad Song
   (1968)
You've Met Your Match (1968)
Chautauqua (1969)
Almost (1969)
Signs of the Zodiac (1969)
It's Hurtin' Time (1969)
Don't Mention My Name (1969)
Change of Habit (1970)
Let Us Pray (1970)
Have a Happy (1970)
Twenty Days and Twenty Nights
   (1970)
I'll Never Know (1971)
Cindy, Cindy (1971)
Where Did I Go Wrong? (1972)
It All Seems to Fall into Line
   (1973)
Rock It (1973)
Picture Portrait (1973)
Lonely Holiday (1973)
That's My World (1973)
Empty the Cup (1973)
We Can Grow (1973)
I Came Home to an Empty Heart
   (1974)
Love in the Afternoon (1974)
Take It or Leave It (1975)
I Love Makin' Love to You
   (1975)
Early Morning Sunshine (1975)
Turn It Around in Your Mind
   (1975)
Blue Summer Rain (1975)
You Can Do It (1977)
Touch That Feeling (1977)
As We Fall in Love Once More
   (1977)
Blue Stars (1978)
The Bunny Hop* (1978)
The Prayer Man's Wagon (1978)

Love Is What You Find (1978)
Lady of the Night (1978)
Gives You the Power (1978)
Get Up (1978)
I Don't Want to Let It Go (1978)
Brain Damage (1979)
I Can't Wait for You (1979)
Keep My Lovelight Burnin'
   (1979)
Keep Your Ear to the Street
   (1979)
You Sho' Look Good to Me
   (1979)
Street Talkin' Survivor (1979)
(Getting Off) On the Hot Line
   (1979)
Love Machine* (1979)
Ocean of Love (1979)
Take a Little Love (1979)
Concerto for Elvis (a symphonic
   work) (1987)

**Wheeler, Susaine P., with
   Marguerite W. Bosley and
   Dorothy L. Knodel**

Our V for Victory (1942)

Williams, Lewis J.

Dear Little Pal
Little Dutch Lunch
Nora Machree
Why Don't Santa Claus Come
   Here?

**Williams, Lewis J., with Paul
   Marienthal**

Brother Bill (1912)

**Zander, Archie. *See Roeser, Harold,
   with Archie Zander***

APPENDIX FOUR

Partial List of Tin Pan Alley Music by Songwriters Who Lived Near Saginaw

These songs were written by people who lived less than twenty miles from Saginaw, but not in the immediate Saginaw metropolitan area. The community where each songwriter lived is listed in parentheses, immediately after his or her name.

DeRemer, Harold, with Bonnie Foster (Bay City)
Flame of My Heart (1928)

DeRemer, Harold, with Thelma Kiger (Bay City)
Ev'ry Day (1928)
Grey Dawn (1928)
It Won't Be Long Now (1928)

de Varennes, Anna M. (Bay City)
Oh You Tigers (1909)
Valse Rose (1912)

Draper, Edward J. B., with G. Bruce Richardson (Bay City)
The Michigan Boys in Blue (1898)

Goulet–Brown, Rosa (Kawkawlin)
Near That Dear Old Fashioned Home upon the Hill (1931)

Hogan, William (Burt)
We Are Bound to Get the Kaiser (1917)

Jay, Harry, with Olive Marjory E. Welcolm (Bay City)
Some Day Far Away in California (1929)

APPENDIX FIVE

Songs about the Saginaw Area (listed alphabetically by title)

Boys of the Winning Team (1909)
Joseph H. Hughes

By the Beautiful Old Saginaw (1909)
*Lewis E. Hurst and Mamie A.
Harper*

Don't You Wish You Were Back
Home Again?* (1913)
Charles K. Harris

East Saginaw Grand March (1888?)
Charles M. Norris

Eddy Band March (1952)
Joseph Cherniavsky

Light Infantry March and
Two-Step** (1894)
Harry Turner

I'm Going Back to That Old Town
(1914)
Joseph H. Hughes

The Lights of My Home Town*
(1915)
Charles K. Harris

Michigan Marches On (1937)
Carl Rupp

Queen of the Saginaw Valley (1907)
Albert W. Platte

Rifle Waltzes*** (1876)
Henry B. Roney

Riverside Park Reverie
John Prindle Scott

Saginaw (1922)
Phebe Callaghan

Saginaw Carnival March (1898)
Alfred W. Norris

Saginaw, My Saginaw
Arthur D. Amsden

Saginaw Street Fair March (1898?)
Alfred W. Norris

There Never Was a Place Like
Saginaw (1949)
Gerald Marks

We Fell in Love on Ojibway Island
(1953)
Joseph Cherniavsky

*Although Harris does not mention
Saginaw specifically in the lyrics,
Saginaw doubtless played a part in
influencing his writing these
songs.

**Dedicated to the Saginaw Light
Infantry.

***Dedicated to the East Saginaw
Rifles.

APPENDIX SIX
SAGINAW'S TOP FORTY

These are forty of the most popular songs of Tin Pan Alley written by people who lived in Saginaw. The songs are listed in the order in which they were published.

After the Ball (1892)
Charles K. Harris

Break the News to Mother (1897)
Charles K. Harris

'Mid the Green Fields of Virginia (1898)
Charles K. Harris

Hello, Central, Give Me Heaven (1901)
Charles K. Harris

Would You Like to Take a Walk with Me? (1908)
Joseph Hughes and Fred Cummins

The Finest Flag That Flies (1914)
Joseph Hughes and Harry Richardson

Down among the Sheltering Palms (1915)
James Brockman

Frisco's Chinatown (1916)
Isham Jones and Olaf "Ole" Olsen

We're in the Army Now (1917)
Isham Jones and Olaf "Ole" Olsen

I'm Forever Blowing Bubbles (1919)
James Brockman

Feather Your Nest (1920)
James Brockman

Wishing (1920)
Isham Jones

Toot, Toot, Tootsie, Goo'Bye (1921)
Danny Russo

On the Alamo (1922)
Isham Jones

Swingin' down the Lane (1923)
Isham Jones

You're Just a Dream Come True (1924)
Isham Jones

I'll See You in My Dreams (1924)
Isham Jones

Never Again (1924)
Isham Jones

It Had to Be You (1924)
Isham Jones

Spain (1924)
Isham Jones

The One I Love Belongs to Somebody Else (1924)
Isham Jones

Sleepy Time Gal (1925)
Ange Lorenzo

Footloose (1925)
Carl Rupp

I'd Walk a Million Miles (To Be a Little Bit Nearer to You) (1927)
Gerald Marks

All of Me (1931)
Gerald Marks

You're the One, You Beautiful Son-of-a-Gun (1931)
Gerald Marks

(With You on My Mind, I Find) I Can't Write the Words (1931)
Gerald Marks

I'll Never Have to Dream Again (1932)
Isham Jones

The Wooden Soldier and the China Doll (1932)
Isham Jones

You've Got Me Crying Again (1933)
Isham Jones

That's What I Want for Christmas (1935)
Gerald Marks

Is It True What They Say about Dixie? (1936)
Gerald Marks

There Is No Greater Love (1936)
Isham Jones

The Aussies and the Yanks Are Here (1942)
John Nauer

Dig Down Deep (1942)
Gerald Marks

It Must Be Jelly ('Cause Jam Don't Shake Like That) (1942)
John Chalmers "Chummy" MacGregor

My Best to You (1942)
Isham Jones

Have a Little Sympathy (1949)
Ben Weisman

Paper Roses (1952)
Ben Weisman

Honey in the Horn (1953)
Ben Weisman

APPENDIX SEVEN

A Partial List of Saginaw Music Publishers: 1871–1940

It was a common practice for unknown songwriters to publish their own songs during the early years of Tin Pan Alley and before. This facilitated good local exposure of the song, while providing the songwriter with attractive copies to take to major publishers, in the hope of being discovered. Below are several Saginaw music publishers and their years of operation.

A. W. Norris (1898)

A. W. Wheat (1872)

Arthur Amsden (1918–1924)

B. F. Reed (1912)

Barrows Music House (1893)

C. M. Norris (1894–1895)

Catterfield Publishing Company (1909)

Clarence Corbit (1926)

Dan Russo (1915)

Doty and Northrup (1921)

Ernest Miller (1932)

Frank H. Erd (1890)

H. J. Norris (1900)

Hughes and Cummins (1908)

J. B. Jackson (1871)

Jones Bros. Music Publishing Company (1915)

Joseph H. Hughes Publishing Company (1910–1918)

Kremer Music Publishing House (1929)

Michigan Music Publishing Company (1914–1916)

N. S. Lagatree (1900)

Peerless Music Publishing Company (1906)

Saginaw Printing and Publishing Company (1907)

Tyler Bros. and Company (1872)

Vervoort and Company (1940)

Williams Song Publishing Company (1912)

BIBLIOGRAPHY

American Society of Composers, Authors, and Publishers. *ASCAP Biographical Dictionary*. New York: Jacques Cattell Press, 1980.

Burton, Jack. *The Blue Book of Tin Pan Alley*. Watkins Glen, N.Y.: Century House, 1962.

Chilton, John. *Who's Who of Jazz*. Philadelphia: Chilton Book Company, 1972.

Clancy, William D., with Audree D. Kenton. Woody Herman—*Chronicles of the Herds*. New York: Schirmer Books, 1995.

Cohen-Stratyner, Barbara, ed. *Popular Music, 1900–1919*. Detroit: Gale Research, 1988.

Craig, Warren. *Sweet and Lowdown*. Metuchen, N.J.: Scarecrow Press, 1978.

Deffaa, Chip. "Composer's Spotlight on Gerald Marks." *Sheet Music*, January/February, 1990.

Dichter, Harry, and Elliot Shapiro. *Handbook of Early American Sheet Music*. New York: Dover, 1977.

Ewen, David. *All the Years of American Popular Music*. Englewood, Cliffs, N.J.: Prentice-Hall, 1977.

————. *American Popular Songs*. New York: Random House, 1966.

————. *Popular American Composers*. New York: H. W. Wilson Company, 1962.

Geller, James J. *Famous Songs and Their Stories*. New York: The Macauly Company, 1931.

————. "Mayhem, in Three-Quarter Time." *The New Republic*, October 15, 1956.

Hamm, Charles. *Yesterdays: Popular Song in America*. New York: W. W. Norton, 1979.

Harris, Charles K. *After the Ball*. New York: Frank-Maurice, 1926.

Hirschhorn, Clive. *The Hollywood Musical*. New York: Crown, 1981.

Hitchcock, H. Wiley, and Stanley Sadie, eds. *The New Grove Dictionary of American Music*. London: Macmillan, 1986.

Husock, Howard. "Popular Song." *The Wilson Quarterly*, Summer, 1988.

Jasen, David A., and Trebor J. Tichenor. *Rags and Ragtime*. New York: Dover, 1978.

Kinkle, Roger D. *The Complete Encyclopedia of Popular Music and Jazz, 1900–1950*. New Rochelle, N.Y.: Arlington House, 1974.

Lax, Roger, and Frederick Smith. *The Great Song Thesaurus*. New York: Oxford University Press, 1984.

Mattfield, Julius. *Variety Music Cavalcade*. Englewood Cliffs, N.J.: Prentice-Hall, 1971.

Mills, James Cooke. *History of Saginaw County Michigan*. Saginaw: Seeman and Peters, 1918.

Saginaw News. October 19, 1947; March 21, 1948; May 19, 1949.

Schuller, Gunther. *The Swing Era.* New York: Oxford University Press, 1989.

Shapiro, Nat, and Bruce Pollack, eds. *Popular Music, 1920–1979.* Detroit: Gale Research, 1985.

Simon, George T. *The Big Bands.* New York: Macmillan, 1967.

———. *The Big Bands Songbook.* New York: Barnes and Noble Books, 1975.

Spaeth, Sigmund. *A History of Popular Music in America.* New York: Random House, 1948.

———. *Read 'Em and Weep.* New York: Arco, 1945.

Walker, Leo. *The Big Band Almanac.* New York: Da Capo Press, 1978.

———. *The Wonderful Era of the Great Dance Bands.* Garden City, N.Y.: Doubleday, 1972.

Wenzel, Lynn, and Carol J. Binkowski. *I Hear America Singing.* New York: Crown, 1989.

Whitcomb, Ian. *After the Ball.* New York: Simon and Schuster, 1972.

———. *Tin Pan Alley.* New York: Simon and Schuster, 1975.

Wilder, Alec. *American Popular Song.* New York: Oxford University Press, 1972.

SUGGESTED ADDITIONAL READING

Clark, Donald. *The Rise and Fall of Popular Music*. New York: St. Martin's Press, 1995.

Clark, Donald, ed. *The Penguin Encyclopedia of Popular Music*. London: Penguin Books, 1990.

Crowther, Bruce, and Mike Pinfold. *The Big Band Years*. New York: Facts on File Publications, 1988.

Ewen, David. *Songs of America*. Chicago: Ziff-Davis, 1947.

———. *The Story of Jerome Kern*. New York: Henry Holt, 1953.

Fernett, Gene. *A Thousand Golden Horns*. Midland, Mich.: The Pendell Company, 1966.

Fremont, Robert A., ed. *Favorite Songs of the Nineties*. New York: Dover, 1973.

Goldman, Herbert G. *Jolson: The Legend Comes to Life*. New York: Oxford University Press, 1988.

Gross, Stuart D. *Saginaw—A History of the Land and the City*. Woodland Hills, Calif.: Windsor Publications, 1980.

Howard, John Tasker. *Our American Music*. New York: Thomas Y. Crowell, 1965.

McCarthy, Albert. *Big Band Jazz*. New York: Berkley Publications, 1974.

———. *The Dance Band Era*. Radnor, Penn.: Chilton Book Company, 1971.

Morris, Joan, and William Bolcom. *After the Ball*. Melville, N.Y.: Mills Publishing Company, 1975.

Simon, George T. *Glenn Miller and His Orchestra*. New York: Thomas Y. Crowell, 1974.

———. *Simon Says—The Sights and Sounds of the Swing Era: 1935–1955*. New York: Galahad Books, 1971.

INDEX

TITLES IN THE
GREAT LAKES BOOKS SERIES

Beyond the Model T: The Other Ventures of Henry Ford, by Ford R. Bryan, 1990

Life after the Line, by Josie Kearns, 1990

Michigan Lumbertowns: Lumbermen and Laborers in Saginaw, Bay City, and Muskegon, 1870–1905, by Jeremy W. Kilar, 1990

Detroit Kids Catalog: The Hometown Tourist by Ellyce Field, 1990

Waiting for the News, by Leo Litwak, 1990 (reprint)

Detroit Perspectives, edited by Wilma Wood Henrickson, 1991

Life on the Great Lakes: A Wheelsman's Story, by Fred W. Dutton, edited by William Donohue Ellis, 1991

Copper Country Journal: The Diary of Schoolmaster Henry Hobart, 1863–1864, by Henry Hobart, edited by Philip P. Mason, 1991

John Jacob Astor: Business and Finance in the Early Republic, by John Denis Haeger, 1991

Survival and Regeneration: Detroit's American Indian Community, by Edmund J. Danziger, Jr., 1991

Steamboats and Sailors of the Great Lakes, by Mark L. Thompson, 1991

Cobb Would Have Caught It: The Golden Years of Baseball in Detroit, by Richard Bak, 1991

Michigan in Literature, by Clarence Andrews, 1992

Under the Influence of Water: Poems, Essays, and Stories, by Michael Delp, 1992

The Country Kitchen, by Della T. Lutes, 1992 (reprint)

The Making of a Mining District: Keweenaw Native Copper 1500–1870, by David J. Krause, 1992

Kids Catalog of Michigan Adventures, by Ellyce Field, 1993

Henry's Lieutenants, by Ford R. Bryan, 1993

Historic Highway Bridges of Michigan, by Charles K. Hyde, 1993

Lake Erie and Lake St. Clair Handbook, by Stanley J. Bolsenga and Charles E. Herndendorf, 1993

Queen of the Lakes, by Mark Thompson, 1994

Iron Fleet: The Great Lakes in World War II, by George J. Joachim, 1994

Turkey Stearnes and the Detroit Stars: The Negro Leagues in Detroit, 1919–1933, by Richard Bak, 1994

Pontiac and the Indian Uprising, by Howard H. Peckham, 1994 (reprint)

Charting the Inland Seas: A History of the U.S. Lake Survey, by Arthur M. Woodford, 1994 (reprint)

Ojibwa Narratives of Charles and Charlotte Kawbawgam and Jacques LePique, 1893–1895. Recorded with Notes by Homer H. Kidder, edited by Arthur P. Bourgeois, 1994, co-published with the Marquette County Historical Society

Strangers and Sojourners: A History of Michigan's Keweenaw Peninsula, by Arthur W. Thurner, 1994

Win Some, Lose Some: G. Mennen Williams and the New Democrats, by Helen Washburn Berthelot, 1995

Sarkis, by Gordon and Elizabeth Orear, 1995

The Northern Lights: Lighthouses of the Upper Great Lakes, by Charles K. Hyde, 1995 (reprint)

Kids Catalog of Michigan Adventures, second edition, by Ellyce Field, 1995

Rumrunning and the Roaring Twenties: Prohibition on the Michigan–Ontario Waterway, by Philip P. Mason, 1995

In the Wilderness with the Red Indians, by E. R. Baierlein, translated by Anita Z. Boldt, edited by Harold W. Moll, 1996

Elmwood Endures: History of a Detroit Cemetery, by Michael Franck, 1996

Master of Precision: Henry M. Leland, by Mrs. Wilfred C. Leland with Minnie Dubbs Millbrook, 1996 (reprint)

Haul-Out: New and Selected Poems, by Stephen Tudor, 1996

Kids Catalog of Michigan Adventures, third edition, by Ellyce Field, 1997

Beyond the Model T: The Other Ventures of Henry Ford, revised edition, by Ford R. Bryan, 1997

Young Henry Ford: A Picture History of the First Forty Years, by Sidney Olson, 1997 (reprint)

From Saginaw Valley to Tin Pan Alley: Saginaw's Contribution to American Popular Music, 1890–1955, by R. Grant Smith, 1997